TEXTBOOK OF

Understanding Universal Human Values

(FIRST EDITION)

By

Shalom Akhai (First Author)
Department of Mechanical Engineering,
Maharishi Markandeshwar Engineering College, Maharishi Markandeshwar (Deemed to be University), Mullana, Ambala, Haryana – 133207, India.

Abhishek Chauhan (Co - Author)
Department of Mechanical Engineering,
Panjab University SSG Regional Centre,
Hoshiarpur 146021, Punjab, India.

Arti Chouksey (Co- Author)
Department of Civil Engineering,
Deenbandhu Chhotu Ram University of Science and Technology, Murthal, Sonipat, Haryana, 131039, India.

Expert Notes, Publisher
Karnal (Haryana)-132001
Visit Us at www.expertnotes.in.

Understanding Universal Human Values

Karnal (Haryana)-132001

www.expertnotes.in.

Book design by Expert Notes, Publisher

www.expertnotes.in.

ISBN: - 978-93-343-0063-5

(E-Book)

ISBN: - 978-93-343-0063-5 (E-Book)

Book design by Cover Designer

www.expertnotes.in

Published by Expert Notes, Publisher

Karnal (Haryana)-132001

www.expertnotes.in

Preface

In an age marked by rapid technological advancement, global connectivity, and material abundance, humanity finds itself confronting profound questions about meaning, purpose, and coexistence. While we have achieved significant milestones in science, infrastructure, and economic development, the inner development of individuals and the ethical fabric of societies have often lagged behind. Rising levels of stress, social fragmentation, environmental degradation, and ethical dilemmas reflect an urgent need to re-examine the values guiding our lives.

This book, *Understanding Universal Human Values*, has been conceived as a response to that need. It is built upon the foundational principles of value-based education as introduced in the Universal Human Values curriculum, aiming to facilitate holistic human development through self-exploration, relationship understanding, and harmony with nature. The book provides a structured approach to introspection and ethical living, encouraging students, educators, and professionals alike to explore the fundamental questions of life: *Who am I? What is my role in society? How can I live meaningfully and harmoniously?*

The content is organized across four major units, covering harmony at the level of the individual, the family, society, and nature. Each chapter combines philosophical clarity with practical applications, case studies, and reflective exercises to ensure that understanding is not merely theoretical but becomes a lived experience.

This work is intended for learners from all disciplines and walks of life. Whether you are a student beginning your academic journey or a professional seeking clarity in a complex world, this book will serve as a guide to connect outer success with inner fulfillment.

It is our hope that through the pages of this book, readers will not only understand universal human values but also internalize and embody them in daily life—for themselves, for others, and for a more compassionate and sustainable world.

— *The Authors*

CONTENTS

Chapter 1: The Purpose of Value Education

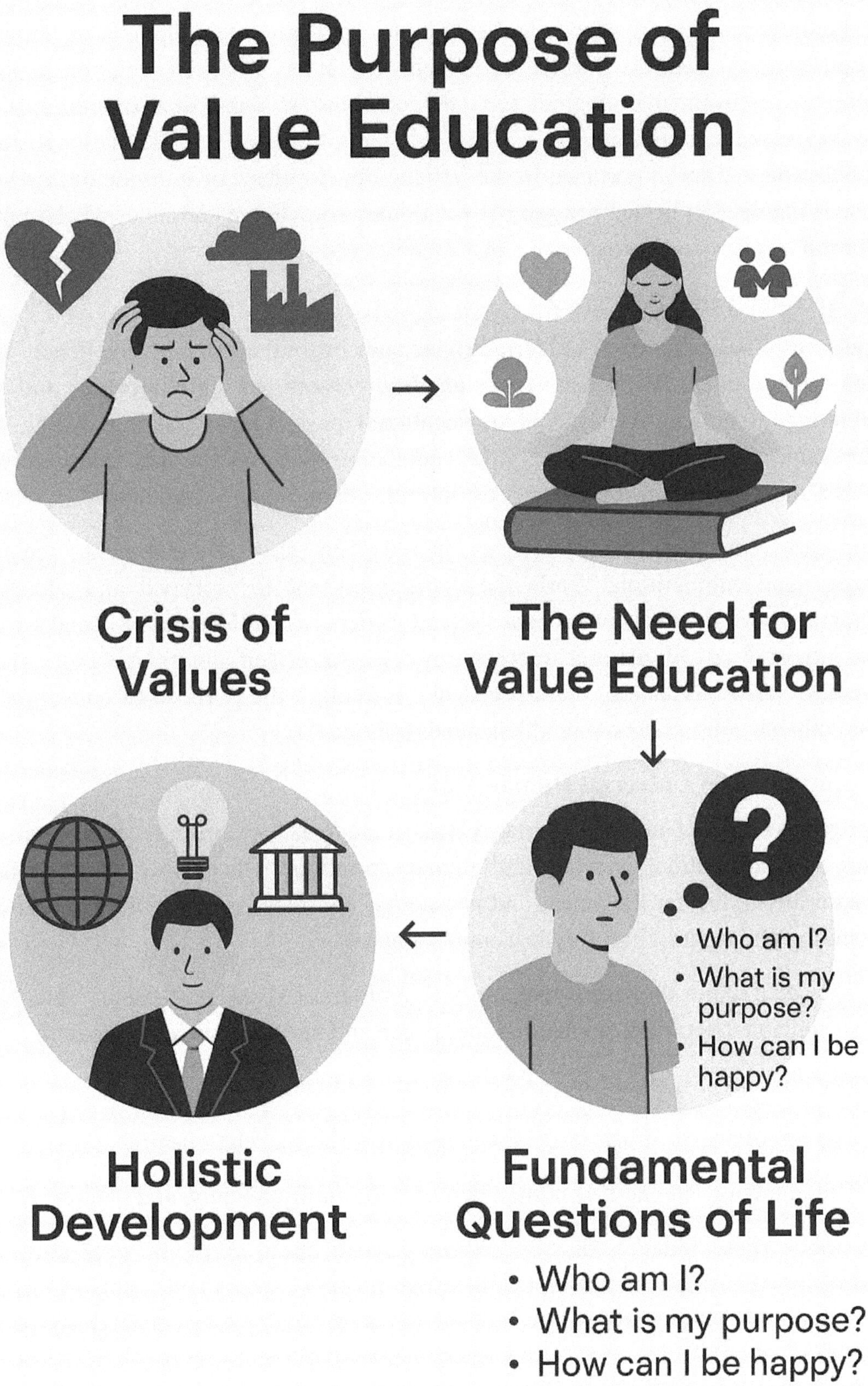

1.1 Introduction

In the modern era, marked by rapid technological progress, industrialization, and material abundance, human society is paradoxically facing a crisis of values. While we have achieved remarkable advancement in science and economics, our inner development as human beings has often lagged behind. Increasing levels of stress, broken relationships, ethical compromises, environmental degradation, and social unrest signal that something essential is missing in our educational approach. This chapter introduces the foundational concept of value education and its importance in the holistic development of individuals and society. It emphasizes the need to bridge the gap between outer knowledge and inner wisdom to foster a life of purpose, peace, and prosperity.

1.2 The Need for Value Education

Value education is an approach to learning that goes beyond academic excellence. It aims to develop moral integrity, social responsibility, emotional intelligence, and a deep understanding of human values. Unlike vocational or technical training, which primarily prepares students for employment, value education nurtures human consciousness and cultivates a sense of responsibility towards oneself, others, society, and nature.

Contemporary education often focuses heavily on skill development, technological proficiency, and competition. While these are important for survival and success in the professional world, they do not necessarily lead to personal fulfillment or social harmony. In fact, the intense focus on material success can often foster selfishness, isolation, and mental health issues. Value education, therefore, seeks to realign the purpose of education towards nurturing ethical, compassionate, and balanced individuals.

1.3 Recapitulation of Universal Human Values - I

In the previous course, Universal Human Values-I, students were introduced to basic concepts of values, self-exploration, harmony, and human aspirations. The central idea was that human beings naturally strive for happiness and prosperity, and these can be achieved through right understanding and right living. Key learnings included:

- The distinction between temporary happiness (based on sensory pleasure) and sustainable happiness (rooted in inner peace and harmonious relationships).
- The concept of natural acceptance and self-verification.
- The importance of trust, respect, and responsibility in relationships.
- The interconnectedness of human beings with family, society, and nature.

Building upon these foundations, this chapter revisits these concepts to create a stronger framework for deeper exploration and application in life.

1.4 Education: The Real Purpose

The primary objective of education should be to facilitate the holistic development of an individual—intellectually, emotionally, socially, and spiritually. An educated person is not only knowledgeable but also wise, responsible, and ethically grounded. The real purpose of education includes:

- Understanding oneself and others
- Living in harmony with the environment
- Developing a vision for a happy and prosperous society
- Cultivating ethical and moral values in everyday life
- Becoming competent in solving real-life problems while upholding human values

In this context, education is not merely a means to an end (such as employment or status), but an ongoing journey of self-growth and social contribution.

1.5 The Gap in Conventional Education

The current education system, while robust in terms of content delivery and testing mechanisms, often lacks a human-centric approach. There is minimal emphasis on understanding the self, cultivating empathy, or exploring life's deeper meaning. As a result, students may emerge from academic programs with degrees but without clarity on how to live meaningfully or relate constructively to others.

Several indicators reflect this gap:

- Growing incidence of student anxiety and depression
- Rising cases of unethical behavior in professional settings
- Social fragmentation and intolerance
- Environmental neglect and unsustainable lifestyles

These issues highlight the urgent need for an educational model that integrates human values as a core component.

1.6 Fundamental Questions of Life

Value education prompts students to engage with fundamental questions that shape human existence:

- Who am I? What is my purpose?
- What is the nature of happiness and how can it be sustained?
- How can I live in harmony with others and with nature?

- What is the role of knowledge in my life?

Such questions, while often overlooked in conventional curricula, are essential for developing a clear understanding of the self and the world. They lead to self-awareness, purposeful living, and informed decision-making.

1.7 The Role of Self-Exploration

Self-exploration is a critical process in value education. It involves examining one's beliefs, thoughts, emotions, and behavior to gain deeper insight into one's own nature and aspirations. The key tools for self-exploration are:

- Natural Acceptance: An innate understanding or feeling of what is right, true, and acceptable to the self
- Experiential Validation: Verifying insights through one's own experience rather than blind belief or hearsay

Self-exploration encourages students to reflect on their lives, understand their motivations, and align their actions with their inner values. It transforms education into a transformative experience rather than a passive accumulation of information.

1.8 Values and Human Aspirations

Human beings universally aspire for happiness (a state of inner well-being) and prosperity (adequate physical resources to live comfortably). These aspirations are not limited by age, culture, or geography. However, the means of achieving them can differ widely based on one's understanding.

Values such as truth, love, peace, compassion, responsibility, and respect act as guiding principles that help fulfill these aspirations in a sustainable manner. When individuals internalize these values, they are more likely to make choices that lead to genuine fulfillment and contribute positively to society.

1.9 The Process of Value Education

Value education is not about imposing rules or moral codes. It is a participative, dialogical, and reflective process. The key components include:

- Dialogue-based Learning: Encouraging discussion and mutual learning
- Experiential Reflection: Relating values to real-life situations
- Continuous Evaluation: Self-assessment and peer feedback
- Practice and Reinforcement: Applying values in everyday decisions

The educator's role is that of a facilitator who guides students to discover and validate values through introspection and interpersonal interactions.

1.10 Benefits of Value Education

Implementing value education in the academic environment yields numerous benefits:

- Enhanced self-awareness and emotional intelligence
- Improved relationships with peers, teachers, and family
- Greater clarity of purpose and life direction
- Ethical decision-making and professional integrity
- Increased sensitivity towards social and ecological issues

These benefits collectively contribute to creating well-rounded individuals who can lead balanced and meaningful lives.

1.11 Practice Session: Natural Acceptance vs. Liking-Disliking

This session encourages students to differentiate between their innate acceptance of certain values and the arbitrary preferences shaped by social conditioning or temporary emotions. For example:

- Natural acceptance may tell us that honesty is right, even if lying might seem advantageous in the short term.
- We may dislike someone due to a personal bias, but naturally accept that every individual deserves respect.

Activity:

- Reflect on situations where you acted based on liking/disliking and compare them with decisions based on your inner sense of rightness.
- Group discussion: Share examples and insights from these reflections.

Objective: To help students recognize the inner compass of natural acceptance and its superiority over superficial preferences.

1.12 Summary

This chapter set the stage for the Universal Human Values course by laying out the rationale for value education. It emphasized the urgent need for integrating values into the education system to address personal, social, and ecological challenges. Through self-exploration, understanding human aspirations, and recognizing the role of natural acceptance, students begin their journey toward a more conscious and meaningful life. The next chapters will delve deeper into these themes, focusing on harmony within the self, in relationships, and with nature.

Chapter 2: Self-Exploration: A Path to Inner Clarity

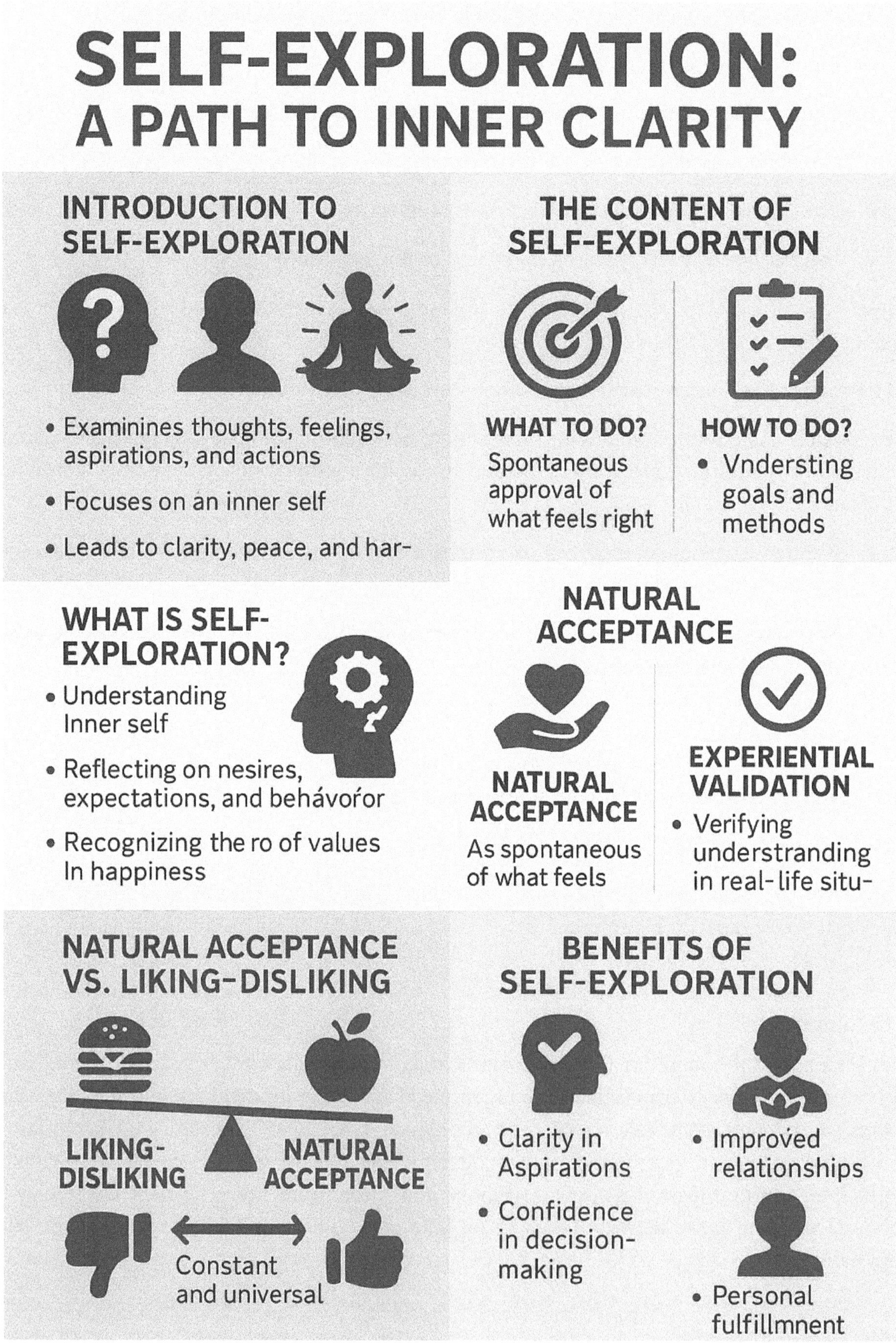

2.1 Introduction to Self-Exploration

Self-exploration is the foundational process in the journey of understanding Universal Human Values. It is the method through which an individual examines their thoughts, feelings, aspirations, and actions to discover the innate nature of the self. Unlike external education that focuses on acquiring information, self-exploration is an inward journey that leads to clarity, peace, and harmony. It helps us discover who we truly are, what we really want, and how we can achieve lasting happiness and prosperity in a just and sustainable way.

2.2 What is Self-Exploration?

Self-exploration is the process of investigating and understanding the inner self. It involves reflecting on one's desires, thoughts, expectations, and behaviorin order to identify whether they are guided by natural acceptance or influenced by external factors like peer pressure, media, or societal norms.

It is not based on mere belief, imagination, or imitation. Instead, it is a methodical process of discovering the truth about oneself and life through experiential validation. Through self-exploration, one becomes capable of:

- Recognizing the difference between needs of the self and needs of the body
- Understanding the role of values in achieving happiness
- Making decisions that are aligned with long-term well-being

2.3 The Content of Self-Exploration

The content of self-exploration revolves around understanding the human being, human aspirations, and the means to fulfill them harmoniously. It involves two key aspects:

1. What to do? (Understanding the right goal or value)
2. How to do? (Understanding the appropriate program or method to achieve that goal)

For example, we all want to be happy. But how do we achieve it? By reflecting on our experiences, we begin to recognize which actions lead to temporary pleasure and which bring sustainable joy. Thus, self-exploration helps in distinguishing between right and wrong, real and superficial.

2.4 The Process of Self-Exploration

The process of self-exploration is fundamentally experiential and dialogical. It involves two key mechanisms:

- **Natural Acceptance**: This is the spontaneous and innate approval of what feels inherently right to us. It is not imposed externally but is naturally agreeable to the self. For instance, we all naturally accept trust in relationships and harmony with nature.
- **Experiential Validation**: This means verifying the understanding gained through natural acceptance by applying it in real-life situations and observing the outcomes.

This combination ensures that our understanding is not only rational but also grounded in personal experience.

2.5 Natural Acceptance vs. Liking-Disliking

Natural acceptance is different from preferences or likes and dislikes, which can vary based on time, place, and circumstances. For example:

- We may like fast food, but naturally accept that healthy food is better for the body.
- We may dislike a person based on misunderstanding, but naturally accept that respect for every human being is right.

Natural acceptance is constant and universal, whereas likes/dislikes are changeable and subjective.

2.6 Characteristics of Natural Acceptance

- **Innate**: It is present within every human being.
- **Universal**: It is the same for all human beings across cultures and regions.
- **Non-contradictory**: It does not create conflict within or with others.
- **Self-verifiable**: It can be validated through personal experience.

Recognizing these characteristics helps in trusting our inner voice and aligning our life with it.

2.7 Self-Verification through Experience

Experiential validation allows us to test our understanding in real-world situations. For example:

- If we believe that helping others brings joy, we can verify it by engaging in an act of kindness and observing how it affects our state of mind.
- If we accept that anger leads to disturbance, we can observe our own experiences to validate the understanding.

This process builds confidence in our inner wisdom and helps us become more self-reliant and peaceful.

2.8 Benefits of Self-Exploration

- **Clarity in Aspirations**: Understanding what truly matters in life
- **Confidence in Decision-making**: Reducing confusion and conflict
- **Improved Relationships**: Acting with empathy, trust, and respect
- **Holistic Development**: Aligning physical, emotional, and intellectual growth
- **Personal Fulfilment**: Living a life with purpose and peace

2.9 Practice Session: Reflecting on Natural Acceptance

Activity 1:

Reflect on the following questions:

- Do I naturally accept being happy or unhappy?
- Do I naturally accept trust or mistrust in relationships?
- Do I naturally accept peace or conflict?
- Do I naturally accept respect or disrespect?

Write down your answers and discuss them in small groups.

Activity 2:

Think of a decision you made recently. Was it based on your natural acceptance or on external influences? How did the outcome affect you emotionally and mentally?

Objective: To help students develop awareness of the difference between natural acceptance and arbitrary choices and to initiate the habit of self-verification.

2.10 Summary

Self-exploration is the gateway to self-awareness, ethical living, and lasting happiness. It helps us connect with our inner voice and live in harmony with ourselves and others. By distinguishing natural acceptance from social conditioning and by validating our understanding through experience, we begin to lead a life that is conscious, compassionate, and fulfilling. This chapter sets the tone for deeper inquiry into the needs of the self and the body, and how to live a balanced life guided by Universal Human Values.

Happiness and Prosperity – Core Human Aspirations

Happiness

Inner satisfaction and well-being

Prosperity

Sufficient physical resources

Key Points

- Happiness is quaitative and subjective
- Prosperity is quantitative and objective
- Both are essential, but their understanding and pursuit must be in harmony

Sensory pleasure is not lasting happiness

Prosperity is beyond accumulation

3.1 Introduction

Human beings across the globe, regardless of their cultural background, religion, nationality, gender, or socioeconomic status, share certain fundamental aspirations. Among these, happiness and prosperity stand out as universal goals that every individual naturally seeks. While people may pursue them through different paths, the essential longing remains the same: a desire to live with inner contentment and material well-being. This chapter delves into the definition, significance, and distinction between happiness and prosperity, analyzes the needs and priorities of human beings, and explores how a right understanding of these core aspirations can lead to a fulfilled and harmonious life.

3.2 Defining Happiness and Prosperity

Happiness refers to a state of inner satisfaction, contentment, and well-being. It is the experience of being in harmony within oneself and with others. Happiness is not momentary pleasure or excitement, but a sustained sense of peace and fulfillment.

Prosperity refers to the condition of having sufficient physical resources to live comfortably. It implies the availability of physical facilities (like food, shelter, clothing, education, healthcare, and transportation) that are required to support a dignified and meaningful life.

Key Points:

- Happiness is qualitative and subjective.
- Prosperity is quantitative and objective.
- Both are essential, but their understanding and pursuit must be in harmony.

3.3 The Distinction between Happiness and Sensory Pleasure

A common misunderstanding is to equate happiness with sensory pleasures such as eating good food, watching movies, traveling, or owning luxury items. While these may provide temporary enjoyment, they are often fleeting and dependent on external stimuli. True happiness, in contrast, arises from within and does not rely on external conditions. It stems from a clear understanding of oneself and living in alignment with inner values.

Examples:

- A person may enjoy a meal but still feel lonely or anxious.
- Someone may own a large house but feel unhappy due to broken relationships.

These examples highlight that while sensory pleasure may offer temporary relief or distraction, it is not a substitute for lasting happiness.

3.4 Prosperity: Beyond Accumulation

Another misconception is equating prosperity with wealth accumulation. People often believe that the more material assets they possess, the more prosperous they are. However, prosperity is not about hoarding; it is about having enough physical resources to meet one's needs and the needs of one's family, with a sense of security and freedom from fear.

Indicators of true prosperity:

- Feeling of abundance rather than lack
- Ability to share and support others
- No anxiety about basic needs
- Conscious consumption and sustainable living

Accumulation, in contrast, may lead to greed, insecurity, competition, and environmental harm.

3.5 Needs of the Self vs. Needs of the Body

Understanding the difference between the needs of the 'self' (the conscious being) and the 'body' (the physical aspect) is crucial.

Needs of the Self ("I"):

- Knowledge
- Peace
- Happiness
- Respect
- Trust

Needs of the Body:

- Food
- Clothing
- Shelter
- Health care
- Physical comfort

The needs of the body are limited, quantifiable, and can be fulfilled with physical facilities. The needs of the self are qualitative, continuous, and can be fulfilled only through right understanding and right feelings.

3.6 Prioritizing Needs and Living in Balance

A common mistake in today's lifestyle is giving undue priority to physical needs while neglecting the inner needs of the self. This imbalance often leads to stress, conflicts, and dissatisfaction.

Balanced Living Includes:

- Providing adequate physical facilities without excess
- Investing time in nurturing relationships
- Pursuing knowledge and self-awareness
- Engaging in meaningful work
- Taking care of physical and mental health

3.7 Misaligned Priorities in Contemporary Society

In many cases, modern life promotes values that place material success above personal fulfillment and ethical living. The culture of consumerism, competitive education, and careerism often misguides individuals toward a one-dimensional pursuit of prosperity at the cost of happiness.

Common Symptoms:

- People with high income but low contentment
- Families with modern comforts but lack of communication
- Technological progress coexisting with mental health crises

3.8 Consequences of the Misunderstanding

- **Individually:** Stress, anxiety, loneliness, burnout
- **Socially:** Fragmentation, mistrust, crime, inequality
- **Ecologically:** Over-consumption, pollution, resource depletion

Recognizing these consequences compels us to revisit our understanding of happiness and prosperity and to seek a more sustainable and ethical path.

3.9 Right Understanding: The Key to Fulfillment

Right understanding means having clarity about what we truly aspire for and how to achieve it. It helps us identify real needs from artificial ones, align our actions with our values, and foster relationships based on trust and respect.

Components of Right Understanding:

- Knowing the distinction between self and body
- Understanding the nature of happiness and prosperity

- Clarity on human relationships
- Recognizing the interconnectedness with society and nature

With right understanding, we are better equipped to live purposefully and joyfully.

3.10 The Role of Education in Cultivating Understanding

The purpose of education should be to develop the competence to live with clarity, responsibility, and harmony. Unfortunately, mainstream education often emphasizes knowledge acquisition without a corresponding development of wisdom or ethics.

Value-Based Education Should Include:

- Encouraging self-exploration
- Integrating ethics into curricula
- Promoting service-learning and real-life applications

This alignment prepares students not just for jobs but for life.

3.11 Practice Session: Exploring Aspirations

Activity 1: Personal Reflection

- What does happiness mean to me?
- What does prosperity mean to me?
- Are my actions aligned with these definitions?

Activity 2: Needs Identification

List your daily needs under two categories:

- Needs of the Self
- Needs of the Body

Discuss:

- Which needs are being overemphasized?
- Are there unfulfilled needs of the self?

Activity 3: Group Discussion

- Share a story or incident where you or someone you know experienced happiness or prosperity.
- Was it based on values or material gain?

Objective: To deepen awareness of one's own life patterns and refine understanding of core aspirations.

3.12 Case Studies: Real-Life Insights

Case 1: The Content Engineer

Ravi, an engineer in a reputed firm, earns a good salary. Initially, he believed buying gadgets and traveling were key to happiness. But over time, he felt empty. Through self-reflection and value education, he began volunteering for environmental causes and mentoring students. His happiness grew not through possessions but through purposeful engagement.

Case 2: The Prosperous Farmer

Lakshmi, a rural farmer, owns a modest piece of land. She grows her own food, shares with neighbors, and lives debt-free. Despite having limited income, she feels prosperous. Her clarity on needs and her strong community ties reflect true prosperity.

These stories demonstrate that happiness and prosperity are attainable through awareness and values, not just wealth.

3.13 Happiness and Prosperity in Relationships

Genuine relationships contribute significantly to both happiness and prosperity. A family where trust, care, and respect are foundational creates a nurturing environment for all members.

Attributes of Fulfilling Relationships:

- Mutual trust
- Open communication
- Emotional support
- Shared responsibilities
- Aligned values

Without harmonious relationships, material success feels empty.

3.14 Technology and Aspirations

Technology should serve human well-being, not dominate or misguide aspirations. When used ethically, it can:

- Improve healthcare
- Facilitate education
- Enhance communication
- Support sustainable development

However, overdependence on or misuse of technology can distort our understanding of needs and create artificial desires.

3.15 Pathways to Achieve Happiness and Prosperity

- **Self-awareness:** Knowing one's aspirations
- **Value integration:** Practicing ethics in daily life
- **Community engagement:** Participating in collective well-being
- **Simplicity:** Avoiding overconsumption
- **Gratitude:** Appreciating what one has

These practices help individuals stay aligned with their core aspirations.

3.16 Role of Social Systems

Societal structures like education, healthcare, and governance should support human well-being and sustainable prosperity. Policies and institutions must be designed to:

- Promote equity
- Provide basic needs
- Encourage ethical behavior
- Foster community

When social systems prioritize values, individuals thrive.

3.17 Environmental Balance and Prosperity

True prosperity is not possible without ecological balance. Nature provides all physical facilities, and its sustainability ensures long-term well-being.

Principles for Eco-friendly Prosperity:

- Reduce, reuse, recycle
- Conserve resources
- Support local and organic farming
- Promote renewable energy

Living in harmony with nature ensures both prosperity and planetary health.

3.18 Summary

Happiness and prosperity are universal human aspirations. Understanding them correctly is essential for living a balanced, fulfilling, and ethical life. Happiness stems from inner harmony and relationships, while prosperity arises from having sufficient physical resources. Both must be pursued with right understanding and responsible action. By differentiating between the needs of the self and the body, aligning with natural acceptance, and adopting sustainable lifestyles, individuals can truly flourish. The next chapter will focus on how right understanding can be extended to relationships and physical facilities, ensuring a more meaningful and harmonious existence.

Chapter 4: Right Understanding of Relationships and Facilities

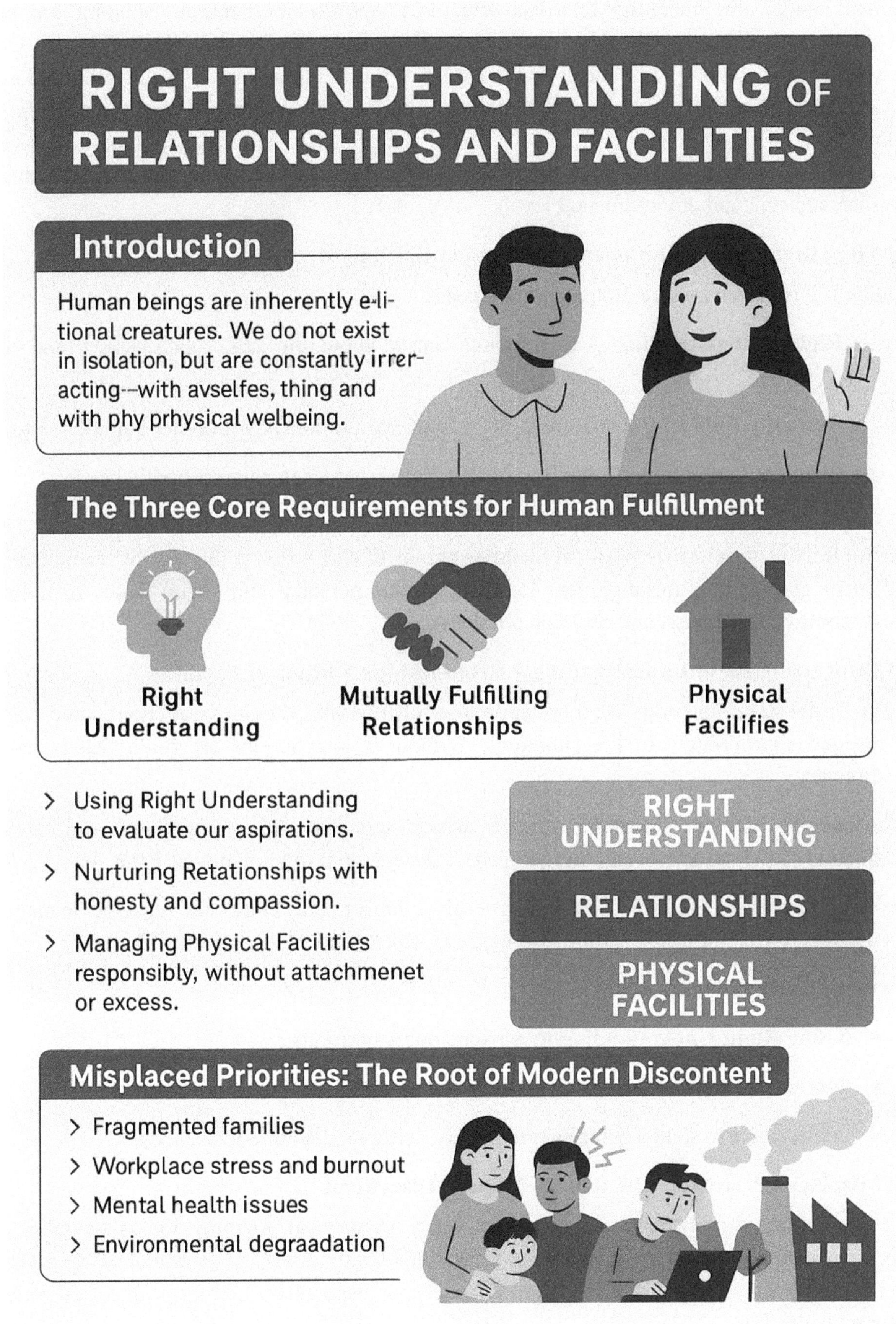

4.1 Introduction

Human beings are inherently relational creatures. We do not exist in isolation but are constantly interacting—with ourselves, with each other, and with the physical world. Our well-being is profoundly influenced by the nature of these interactions. This chapter explores the role of relationships and physical facilities in human life and emphasizes the need for a value-based understanding of both. It investigates the priority these elements should be given and how their right understanding contributes to harmony and fulfillment at the individual, familial, societal, and environmental levels.

4.2 The Three Core Requirements for Human Fulfilment

Human life is driven by three foundational needs:

1. **Right Understanding** – Developing clarity about the self, relationships, and the world.
2. **Mutually Fulfilling Relationships** – Living harmoniously with other human beings.
3. **Physical Facilities** – Availability of material resources to support bodily needs.

While all three are essential, they are often misunderstood or prioritized incorrectly. The general trend is to prioritize physical facilities above all else, often at the cost of relationships and inner clarity. This misalignment leads to various personal and social issues including stress, conflict, loneliness, and ecological imbalance.

4.3 Prioritizing Right Understanding > Relationships > Physical Facilities

Right Understanding forms the foundation of a fulfilled life. It guides our choices and helps us respond appropriately to life situations. Without it, our actions are often reactive and misdirected.

Relationships are the medium through which we experience emotional and social satisfaction. Trust, affection, and mutual respect are essential to human well-being.

Physical Facilities, while necessary for bodily comfort, are finite and must be managed wisely. When overemphasized, they lead to greed, stress, and unsustainable living.

Correct Prioritization means:

- Using **Right Understanding** to evaluate our aspirations.
- Nurturing **Relationships** with honesty and compassion.
- Managing **Physical Facilities** responsibly, without attachment or excess.

4.4 Misplaced Priorities: The Root of Modern Discontent

In contemporary society, there is a heavy emphasis on material accumulation as a symbol of success. From early education to career aspirations, individuals are conditioned to pursue wealth and possessions, often neglecting the deeper aspects of life. This distorted value system results in:

- Fragmented families
- Workplace stress and burnout
- Mental health issues
- Environmental degradation

Examples:

- Families where members are physically present but emotionally distant.
- Professionals earning well but lacking meaningful relationships.
- Societies with advanced technology but increasing inequality and unrest.

4.5 The Nature of Human Relationships

Human relationships are not transactional but intrinsic to our very being. They are not based on utility or profit but on mutual recognition and respect. Relationships flourish when built on the foundation of universal human values such as:

- **Trust** – Assurance in the intentions of others.
- **Respect** – Acknowledging the inherent value of every human being.
- **Affection** – Warmth in interactions.
- **Care** – Concern for others' well-being.
- **Guidance** – Supporting others with clarity and wisdom.
- **Gratitude** – Appreciation for the contributions of others.

Each of these values fulfills a specific aspect of emotional and moral development.

4.6 Challenges to Relationships in Modern Times

- Increasing focus on individualism and personal gain.
- Miscommunication and lack of time spent together.
- Influence of media promoting competition and comparison.
- Unrealistic expectations and conditional acceptance.

These factors often lead to mistrust, conflict, and breakdown of families and communities.

4.7 Developing Right Understanding in Relationships

With the right understanding, we:

- See the other as a human being rather than a role or function.
- Communicate openly and listen without judgment.
- Recognize the difference between intention (always good) and competence (may vary).

This mindset enables us to respond with empathy rather than react with anger or frustration.

4.8 Physical Facilities: Purpose and Limitations

Physical facilities are essential for supporting the needs of the body. However, their usefulness is limited to:

- Providing comfort
- Ensuring health and safety
- Facilitating daily functions

Excessive focus on facilities leads to endless desires, comparison, insecurity, and environmental harm.

Key Points:

- Needs of the body are finite.
- Accumulation does not equate to well-being.
- Conscious consumption supports sustainability.

4.9 Prosperity vs. Accumulation

Prosperity is the feeling of having enough and the capacity to share. It involves accurate assessment of needs and the assurance that those needs will be fulfilled.

Accumulation is the endless gathering of resources beyond one's needs, often driven by fear or comparison.

Indicators of Prosperity:

- Contentment
- Sharing
- Time for relationships
- Minimal anxiety about future needs

Indicators of Accumulation:

- Greed
- Overwork
- Resource hoarding
- Neglect of health and relationships

4.10 Living with the Right Priorities

To live in alignment with our true nature and aspirations, we must:

- Place **Right Understanding** at the center of our life.

- Give importance to **Relationships** as the core of emotional fulfillment.
- Use **Physical Facilities** wisely and sustainably.

Balanced Living Includes:

- Time for self-reflection
- Quality time with family and friends
- Conscious management of finances and possessions
- Engaging in meaningful work that serves others

4.11 The Role of Education in Value Prioritization

Education must go beyond academic excellence and career readiness. It should foster:

- Self-awareness
- Ethical reasoning
- Emotional intelligence
- Social responsibility

When students learn to value relationships and sustainability over material success, they become more balanced and responsible citizens.

4.12 Practice Session: Reflecting on Personal Priorities

Activity 1: Daily Routine Analysis

List your daily activities and identify how much time is spent on:

- Self-growth (e.g., learning, meditation)
- Nurturing relationships (e.g., family time, conversations)
- Pursuing or maintaining physical facilities (e.g., working, shopping)

Activity 2: Personal Reflection

- What do I value the most?
- Does my time investment reflect my values?
- What changes can I make to live more harmoniously?

Activity 3: Group Discussion

- Share experiences of how prioritizing relationships or values improved your well-being.
- Discuss examples where material pursuits led to stress or conflict.

Objective:

To help students develop self-awareness about their life priorities and inspire them to live with balance and purpose.

4.13 Case Studies

Case Study 1: The Successful Executive

Meena is a senior executive in a multinational company. Her work is demanding and well-compensated. However, her personal life is in turmoil—strained relations with her spouse, no time for her children, and constant stress. After attending a value education workshop, she reassessed her priorities. By delegating work, setting boundaries, and investing time in her family, she found renewed happiness and improved health.

Case Study 2: The Village Teacher

Ramesh is a school teacher in a rural village. He earns a modest salary but is deeply respected in his community. He spends his evenings teaching underprivileged children, tends a small farm with his family, and participates in community events. Though he lacks luxury, he lives with a strong sense of prosperity and purpose.

These stories illustrate how right understanding and priority-setting lead to fulfillment, regardless of socioeconomic status.

4.14 Environmental Perspective

Physical facilities, when misused or overexploited, contribute to environmental issues such as:

- Pollution
- Resource depletion
- Climate change

A right understanding encourages sustainable living by:

- Reducing waste
- Valuing simplicity
- Encouraging eco-friendly technologies
- Supporting community-based production

4.15 Social Perspective

In a society where material wealth is overvalued, inequality, exclusion, and social unrest become common. When values guide social behavior:

- Trust increases
- Cooperation thrives
- Justice and equity are promoted

Social systems—education, economy, governance—must be designed to reflect these values.

4.16 Summary

Right understanding of relationships and physical facilities is vital to a harmonious and fulfilling life. Prioritizing clarity and values enables individuals to nurture meaningful relationships and use material resources responsibly. Misplaced priorities often lead to emotional distress, social conflict, and ecological damage. Through introspection, education, and conscious living, we can realign our priorities to create a balanced, ethical, and sustainable way of life. The next chapter will delve deeper into how modern pursuits, driven by misunderstanding, have led to widespread discontent and imbalance.

Chapter 5: A Critical Look at Modern Pursuits

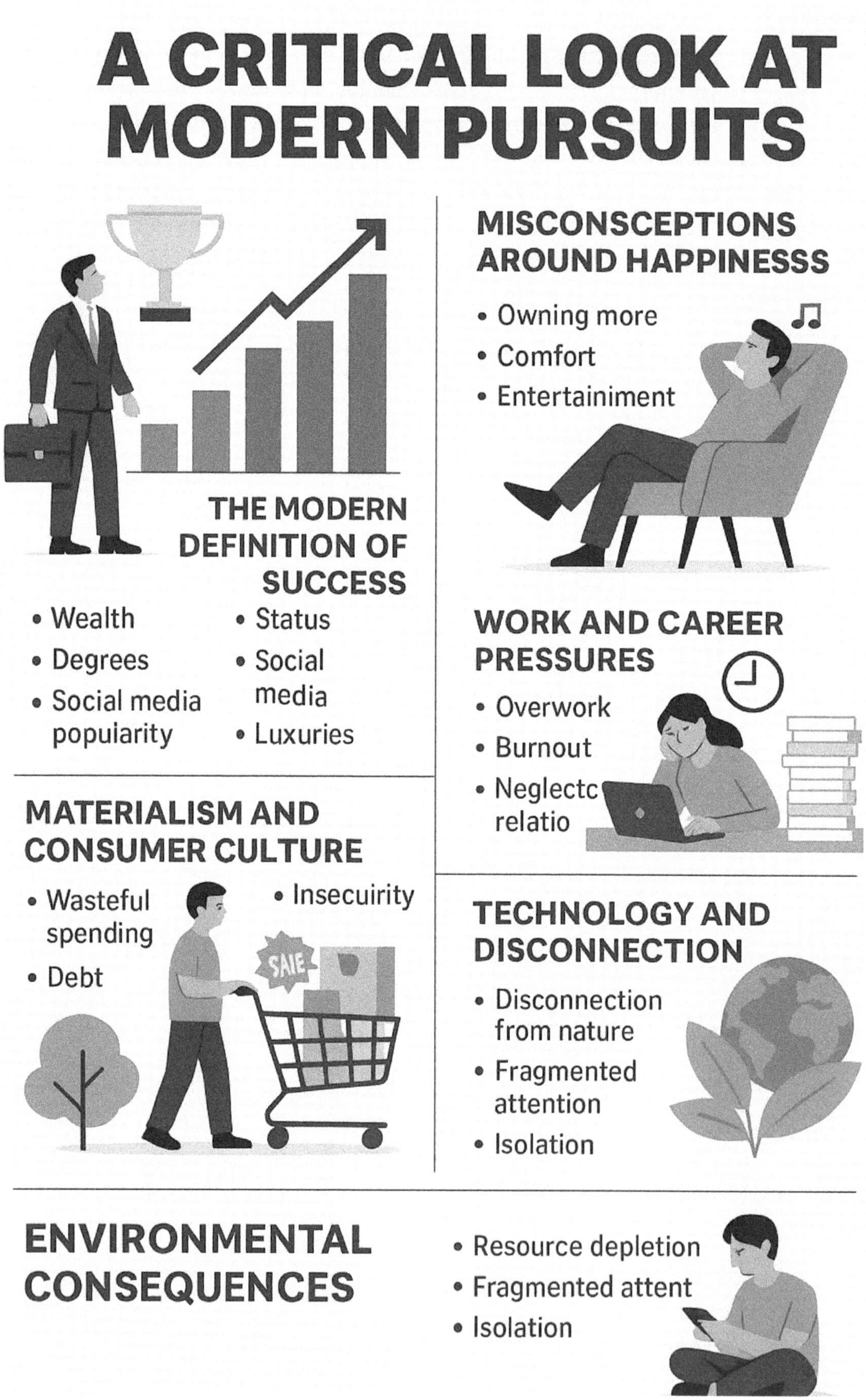

5.1 Introduction

The modern world, with its spectacular scientific, technological, and economic achievements, is often portrayed as a model of progress. However, beneath this glossy surface lies a growing undercurrent of dissatisfaction, confusion, and disconnection. Despite material advancement, issues like mental health disorders, environmental degradation, strained relationships, and societal unrest are on the rise. This chapter critically examines modern pursuits, questioning commonly held assumptions about success, happiness, and prosperity. It aims to provide a deeper understanding of the root causes of this imbalance and offer a value-based perspective to realign human aspirations.

5.2 The Modern Definition of Success

In contemporary society, success is largely defined by material metrics:

- Wealth accumulation
- Career status
- Educational degrees
- Social media popularity
- Possession of luxury goods

While these achievements may offer temporary validation, they do not necessarily equate to happiness or inner fulfillment. A narrow focus on external accomplishments often comes at the cost of inner peace, health, relationships, and social cohesion.

5.3 Misconceptions Around Happiness

Happiness today is frequently confused with pleasure, comfort, or entertainment. The pursuit of happiness has become a pursuit of consumption.

Common Misconceptions:

- Happiness comes from owning more.
- Comfort and luxury guarantee satisfaction.
- Entertainment is equivalent to peace of mind.

These ideas lead to a dependence on external conditions, which are inherently unstable. When our sense of well-being is tied to circumstances beyond our control, we become vulnerable to dissatisfaction, stress, and depression.

5.4 The Pleasure Trap

Modern lifestyles often prioritize sensory pleasures—tasty food, fashionable clothing, digital gadgets, travel, and instant gratification. These activities activate short-term dopamine responses in the brain, creating a cycle of desire and temporary satisfaction. Over time, this leads to:

- Diminished joy from simple things

- Increased craving for stimulation
- Emotional imbalance
- Neglect of deeper needs such as love, trust, and purpose

5.5 Materialism and Consumer Culture

Consumerism thrives on the belief that owning more leads to being more. Advertising, media, and peer influence promote continuous consumption as a path to happiness. This belief system fosters:

- Wasteful spending
- Unnecessary debt
- Environmental harm
- Insecurity and comparison

It also distorts self-worth, tying it to possessions rather than character, contribution, or inner growth.

5.6 Work and Career Pressures

Professional achievement is a major component of modern pursuits. While meaningful work is essential, the obsession with career success often results in:

- Overwork and burnout
- Compromised ethics
- Neglected relationships
- Reduced time for self-care and reflection

Corporate environments may encourage competition over collaboration, leading to unhealthy stress and a loss of personal identity.

5.7 Education as a Commodity

Education today is often viewed as a means to secure employment, social status, or financial gain. As a result:

- Learning becomes test-oriented rather than value-oriented.
- Creativity, curiosity, and moral development are sidelined.
- Students experience high pressure, anxiety, and disengagement.

True education should empower individuals to understand themselves, their relationships, and their responsibilities towards society and nature.

5.8 Social Comparison and the Illusion of Success

Social media platforms have intensified the culture of comparison. Carefully curated images and stories promote:

- Unrealistic standards of beauty, wealth, and success
- Envy and low self-esteem
- Superficial relationships and validation seeking

These distortions distract people from their authentic needs and create emotional instability.

5.9 Technology and Disconnection

Technology has revolutionized communication, work, and entertainment. However, overreliance on it has caused:

- Disconnection from nature and face-to-face relationships
- Attention fragmentation and addiction
- Emotional detachment and isolation

A balanced use of technology is essential to support, not replace, real human experiences.

5.10 Environmental Consequences

Modern pursuits driven by consumption have significant ecological impacts:

- Resource depletion
- Deforestation
- Climate change
- Pollution

The belief that economic growth must be endless leads to unsustainable practices that harm the very ecosystems that support life. There is an urgent need to reframe development in harmony with ecological limits.

5.11 Health and Well-being

Modern lifestyle disorders, such as obesity, diabetes, hypertension, and mental illnesses, are on the rise. These health issues are often rooted in:

- Sedentary habits
- Poor dietary choices
- Stress from overwork and social pressure
- Lack of emotional resilience

A holistic view of health must include physical, mental, emotional, and social well-being.

5.12 Relationship Breakdown

As personal goals become self-centered and materialistic, the quality of relationships declines. Symptoms include:

- Increase in divorce and separation
- Estrangement within families
- Lack of empathy in social behavior

Relationships require time, presence, and emotional investment—qualities often compromised by the modern race for success.

5.13 Redefining Aspirations

Human aspirations are not limited to wealth and recognition. Deeper, universal aspirations include:

- Understanding and harmony within the self
- Loving and respectful relationships
- Meaningful contribution to society
- Sustainable coexistence with nature

Aligning our life with these aspirations provides a foundation for true success and fulfillment.

5.14 Real-Life Contrasts

Case 1: The Corporate Achiever

Raj, a high-ranking executive, owns luxury cars, lives in a posh apartment, and travels frequently. Outwardly, he seems successful. Yet he battles insomnia, high blood pressure, and a sense of emptiness. Despite external success, he feels unfulfilled.

Case 2: The Rural Artisan

Asha, a weaver in a small village, lives modestly but enjoys a strong bond with her family and community. She grows her own food, teaches local children, and sings traditional songs. Her life, though simple, is rich in joy, peace, and contribution.

These examples challenge the conventional idea of what it means to be successful.

5.15 Towards a Holistic Model of Progress

A value-based model of development emphasizes:

- Quality of life over quantity of possessions
- Well-being over wealth
- Ethics over efficiency
- Community over competition

- Sustainability over speed

This requires a shift from ego-driven pursuits to eco-centered lifestyles.

5.16 Role of Value Education

Value education helps individuals:

- Reflect on their aspirations
- Identify true sources of happiness
- Make informed, ethical choices
- Build nurturing relationships
- Live in harmony with nature

By integrating values into personal, educational, and professional life, we can move from blind pursuits to meaningful living.

5.17 Practice Session: Examining Modern Pursuits

Activity 1: Reflection Exercise

- What does success mean to me?
- Who do I admire and why?
- Do my daily activities align with my values?

Activity 2: Lifestyle Analysis

Track your daily screen time, consumption habits, and social interactions for a week. Reflect:

- Are these activities adding value to my life?
- What can I reduce or modify?

Activity 3: Group Discussion

Discuss a real-life example of someone who changed their life after realizing the limitations of modern pursuits.

Objective:
To develop awareness of one's own choices and reframe aspirations around lasting well-being and social contribution.

5.18 Case Studies in Transformation

Case Study 1: From IT to Farming

Sandeep, an IT professional, left his high-paying job to become an organic farmer. His new lifestyle is less lucrative but far more satisfying. He speaks of improved health, stronger family bonds, and a deeper sense of purpose.

Case Study 2: Inner Transformation through Meditation

Anita, a college professor, integrated daily meditation and self-reflection into her routine. She reports reduced stress, better relationships with students, and enhanced clarity in teaching.

These stories demonstrate how shifting priorities leads to greater fulfillment.

5.19 Practical Guidelines for Reorienting Modern Life

- Begin each day with self-reflection or meditation.
- Limit consumption to needs rather than wants.
- Prioritize time for relationships and community.
- Make ethical and sustainable choices in lifestyle and work.
- Redefine success in terms of well-being, contribution, and harmony.

5.20 Summary

Modern pursuits, as commonly understood, often lead to imbalance and discontent. A critical examination reveals that materialism, competition, and ego-centered aspirations contribute to widespread personal, social, and environmental challenges. By revisiting and redefining our understanding of success and happiness, and by integrating human values into every sphere of life, we can transition toward a more balanced, ethical, and fulfilling way of living. The next chapter will explore how living in harmony at multiple levels is the key to achieving these universal human goals.

Chapter 6: Living in Harmony – Pathway to Fulfilment

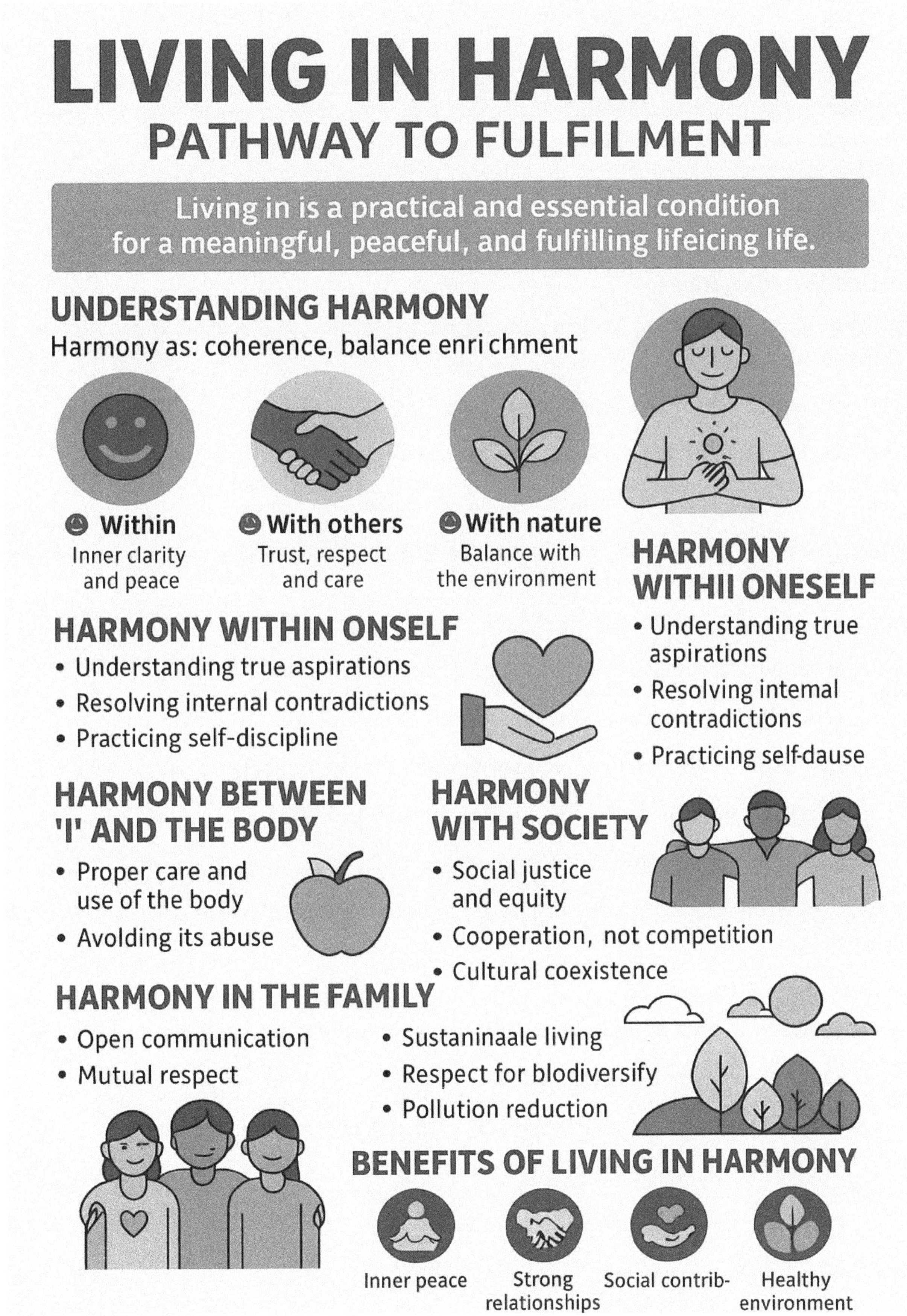

6.1 Introduction

Harmony is not just an abstract ideal; it is a practical and essential condition for living a meaningful, peaceful, and fulfilling life. Living in harmony means aligning oneself with one's values, nurturing healthy relationships, engaging constructively with society, and living sustainably with nature. In this chapter, we will explore what it means to live in harmony at various levels of existence and how such a way of life paves the path toward true human fulfillment. We will examine how the integration of right understanding and ethical action across the individual, familial, societal, and ecological dimensions results in lasting happiness and prosperity.

6.2 Understanding Harmony

Harmony refers to the state of being in coherence, balance, and mutual enrichment. In a human context, it means:

- Within: A state of inner clarity and peace
- With others: Relationships based on trust, respect, and mutual care
- With nature: Living in balance with the environment

Without harmony, life becomes fragmented, stressful, and chaotic. Harmony is not a luxury—it is a necessity for holistic human well-being.

6.3 Levels of Harmony

Living in harmony encompasses various dimensions:

1. **Individual Level**: Harmony within the self ('I') and between 'I' and the body
2. **Family Level**: Harmonious relationships with family members
3. **Societal Level**: Coexistence with the community and society
4. **Nature Level**: Living sustainably and respectfully with the environment

Each of these dimensions is interrelated. Disturbance at any one level can ripple across others.

6.4 Harmony Within Oneself

This is the foundation for all other levels of harmony. It involves:

- Understanding one's true aspirations
- Resolving internal contradictions (e.g., conflict between values and actions)
- Cultivating emotional intelligence
- Practicing self-discipline and mindfulness

When an individual is in harmony within, they experience:

- Clear thinking

- Emotional balance
- Purposeful action

Without inner harmony, external circumstances, no matter how favorable, cannot provide lasting happiness.

6.5 Harmony Between 'I' and the Body

'I' (the conscious self) and the body are two distinct yet interconnected entities. Harmony between the two includes:

- Proper care and nourishment of the body
- Using the body as a tool for expressing human values
- Avoiding abuse (e.g., addictions, overwork)

Examples:

- Eating healthy foods that are appropriate to bodily needs
- Avoiding excessive screen time and promoting physical activity

A disciplined and respectful relationship with the body supports the aspirations of the self.

6.6 Harmony in the Family

Family is the primary social unit where values are learned and practiced. Harmony in the family includes:

- Open and empathetic communication
- Mutual trust and respect
- Sharing responsibilities
- Encouraging growth and individuality

A harmonious family provides emotional security, moral grounding, and support in times of need.

6.7 Common Disruptions in Family Harmony

- Lack of time spent together
- Miscommunication or assumptions
- Value conflicts between generations
- Overemphasis on material provision over emotional needs

Addressing these issues through dialogue, shared activities, and mutual understanding helps restore harmony.

6.8 Harmony in the Society

A harmonious society is characterized by:

- Social justice and equity
- Cooperation rather than competition
- Shared responsibility for the common good
- Cultural appreciation and coexistence

In such a society, individuals are free to pursue their development while contributing positively to others.

6.9 Challenges to Societal Harmony

- Economic inequality
- Discrimination and prejudice
- Political divisiveness
- Breakdown of community bonds

Fostering societal harmony requires inclusive policies, civic education, community dialogue, and an emphasis on shared human values.

6.10 Harmony with Nature

Nature sustains life through complex systems of balance and interdependence. Living in harmony with nature includes:

- Understanding the four orders: material, plant, animal, and human
- Respecting ecological limits
- Reducing pollution and resource waste
- Supporting biodiversity and regenerative practices

Sustainable living is not just about conserving resources; it is about recognizing our place within a greater whole.

6.11 Technology and Harmony

Technology, when guided by values, can enhance harmony:

- Renewable energy reduces environmental harm
- Communication tools can connect people across cultures
- Assistive technologies empower the differently-abled

However, misused or value-neutral technology can create disconnection, pollution, and social alienation.

6.12 Holistic View of Coexistence

The ultimate expression of harmony is **coexistence**—recognizing that all beings are part of an interconnected whole.

Coexistence involves:

- Mutual respect between species
- Recognition of diversity as strength
- Active contribution to shared ecosystems and societies

It is not about uniformity, but about unity in diversity.

6.13 Practice Session: Decision-Making Guided by Harmony

Activity 1: Personal Audit

Reflect on a recent decision:

- Was it aligned with your values?
- Did it benefit others?
- Was it sustainable?

Activity 2: Role Play

Simulate a family or community decision (e.g., planning a festival with minimal environmental impact) and discuss different viewpoints.

Activity 3: Group Dialogue

Discuss:

- How can I contribute to harmony in my class/hostel/institute?
- What actions reflect my responsibility to society and nature?

Objective:
To make students aware of the harmony-oriented lens for everyday decision-making.

6.14 Real-Life Examples of Living in Harmony

Example 1: Eco-Village Model

Villages like Auroville (India) and Findhorn (Scotland) demonstrate how communities can live sustainably through:

- Shared responsibilities
- Renewable energy
- Organic farming
- Education centered around values

Example 2: Corporate Social Innovation

Companies that prioritize stakeholder well-being over profit margins:

- Provide ethical working conditions
- Support community development
- Invest in sustainable technologies

These models reflect how harmony can be integrated into both personal and organizational life.

6.15 Harmony in Professional Life

Living in harmony extends to professional life through:

- Ethical business practices
- Respectful workplace culture
- Purpose-driven careers
- Work-life balance

Professionals who are value-driven contribute more meaningfully and experience less burnout.

6.16 Universal Human Order

The idea of a universal human order envisions:

- Undivided society
- Fearless, trust-based relationships
- Sustainable prosperity for all
- Policies and structures that reflect human values

This is not utopia, but a practical outcome of consistent value-based living.

6.17 Pathways to Cultivate Harmony

- **Self-awareness** through reflection and meditation
- **Dialogue** in families and communities
- **Education** that integrates values at all levels
- **Responsible consumption** of resources
- **Active contribution** to social and ecological causes

6.18 Benefits of Living in Harmony

- Inner peace and mental stability

- Strong and supportive relationships
- Meaningful contribution to society
- Healthy environment and sustainable future

Harmony is not just the result of values—it is also the soil in which they grow.

6.19 Challenges to Harmony and How to Overcome Them

- **Stress and distractions**: Use mindfulness practices to regain clarity
- **Conflicting values**: Engage in respectful dialogue to find common ground
- **Peer pressure**: Rely on natural acceptance over external approval
- **Information overload**: Curate inputs that support holistic well-being

6.20 Summary

Living in harmony is not only an aspiration but a necessity for human fulfillment. It encompasses inner clarity, loving relationships, responsible citizenship, and ecological awareness. When we live harmoniously at all levels—within ourselves, with others, in society, and with nature—we create a foundation for sustainable peace and prosperity. This chapter offered a practical framework and real-life insights into how value-based decision-making leads to integrated and fulfilled living. The journey of value education culminates in the ability to make harmony a way of life, shaping a better future for oneself and for the world.

Chapter 7: Human Being = 'I' + Body – The Dual Nature of Existence

7.1 Introduction

Human beings are often regarded as one unified entity in everyday understanding, but a closer introspection reveals that we are a composite of two distinct yet interrelated realities: the 'I' (conscious self) and the body (material entity). This chapter delves into the dual nature of human existence and presents an in-depth exploration of the roles, characteristics, and interdependence of 'I' and the body. Recognizing this duality not only helps us understand ourselves better but also allows us to live in greater harmony within and with others.

7.2 The Need for Self-Inquiry

In a world driven by external success, appearance, and physical comfort, many people rarely reflect on their inner being. Yet true well-being arises from the integration of the self and the body. The lack of distinction between the two often results in:

- Over-identification with physical appearance
- Stress due to unfulfilled desires
- Disconnection from inner purpose
- Confusion in decision-making

Self-inquiry becomes the first step toward developing a clearer understanding of our true nature.

7.3 The Composition of the Human Being

A human being is a **co-existence** of:

- **'I' (Self, Atman, Consciousness)**
- **The Body (Physical Instrument)**

'I' is the **seer**, **knower**, and **doer** within, whereas the body is the **instrument** through which 'I' expresses itself in the physical world.

Aspect	'I' (Self)	Body
Nature	Conscious, intangible	Material, tangible
Function	Understanding, Desiring, Deciding	Physiological processes
Needs	Happiness, Knowledge, Peace	Food, Shelter, Clothing, Health
Activities	Thinking, Imagining, Reflecting	Breathing, Digestion, Movement
Continuity	Continuous	Temporary
Control	Governs the body	Functions under 'I's direction

Understanding this framework allows us to distinguish the roles of 'I' and the body, thereby enabling better self-regulation and health.

7.4 Characteristics of 'I' (The Self)

- **Existentially continuous**: 'I' exists even when the body is asleep or inactive.
- **Desires meaning and purpose**: Seeks clarity and fulfillment.
- **Reflective**: Capable of questioning and self-awareness.
- **Stable needs**: Needs like trust, love, respect remain constant.

'I' is not visible or measurable in physical terms but is evident in its functioning—through thoughts, desires, and decisions.

7.5 Characteristics of the Body

- **Material entity**: Composed of atoms and molecules.
- **Needs maintenance**: Requires food, rest, hygiene.
- **Perishable**: Subject to ageing, disease, and death.
- **Visible and measurable**: Can be examined through scientific tools.

The body is indispensable for interaction with the physical world but is limited in its intelligence and responsiveness.

7.6 Interdependence of 'I' and Body

Although distinct, 'I' and the body depend on each other for full human functioning:

- 'I' uses the body to communicate, move, and engage with the environment.
- The body depends on 'I' for purposeful direction and self-care.

Example: Hunger is felt in the body, but the decision to eat now or later is made by 'I'.

7.7 Misidentification and Its Consequences

When individuals identify solely with the body:

- They prioritize looks over substance
- Experience fear of death and aging
- Feel insecure and anxious over physical changes

When they ignore the needs of the body:

- They risk health problems, exhaustion, and disease
- Fail to appreciate the body's value as an instrument

Balanced understanding prevents both neglect and obsession.

7.8 The Body as an Instrument of 'I'

Like a vehicle is operated by a driver, the body is operated by the 'I'.

- 'I' decides what to eat; the body digests it.

- 'I' decides where to go; the body performs the action.
- 'I' sets the intention; the body executes it.

This analogy clarifies our responsibility toward both self-awareness and body-care.

7.9 Knowing the 'I' through Self-Observation

We cannot see the 'I' as we see the body, but we can **observe** its functioning:

- **Desires**: What do I want and why?
- **Thoughts**: What am I thinking, and does it align with my values?
- **Expectations**: Are they realistic and value-based?

This inner observation reveals the nature and needs of the self.

7.10 Practice Session: Distinguishing 'I' and Body

Activity 1: Journal Reflection

- List 5 needs of your body.
- List 5 needs of your 'I'.
- Identify any conflict or harmony between them.

Activity 2: Guided Discussion

- Share examples where decisions of 'I' were misaligned with body needs (e.g., overeating, sleep deprivation).

Objective:
To help students practically recognize and balance the dual needs of their existence.

7.11 Role of 'I' in Governance

'I' is the governor, and the body is the governed. Effective governance means:

- Clear thinking
- Right intention
- Discipline and self-control

When 'I' is unclear, distracted, or indulgent, the body suffers. When 'I' is balanced and responsible, the body thrives.

7.12 Relationship with the External World

All our interactions—with people, society, and nature—are mediated through our understanding as 'I'. If 'I' is:

- In harmony, relationships flourish
- In conflict, misunderstandings arise

Thus, clarity within leads to clarity outside.

7.13 Cultural and Philosophical Perspectives

Various traditions affirm the duality of human nature:

- **Indian philosophy**: 'Atman' and 'Sharir' (soul and body)
- **Greek thought**: 'Psyche' and 'Soma' (mind and body)
- **Islamic view**: 'Ruh' (spirit) and 'Jism' (body)
- **Christian theology**: Body and soul distinction

These traditions converge on the importance of aligning inner and outer life.

7.14 Implications for Personal Development

Understanding the self-body relationship helps in:

- Improving self-discipline
- Reducing anxiety and confusion
- Enhancing focus and decision-making
- Achieving balanced growth

7.15 Health, Happiness, and the Self-Body Balance

True health is more than absence of disease; it is harmony between 'I' and body.

- Mental distress often originates from unresolved inner conflicts
- Bodily illness can be prevented by self-care driven by understanding

7.16 Education and Self-Body Awareness

Schools and universities should incorporate:

- Mindfulness training
- Value-based education
- Physical well-being programs integrated with ethical reflection

Such education fosters whole-person development.

7.17 Societal Impact of Self-Body Clarity

When individuals understand and respect their dual nature, society benefits:

- Reduced stress and violence
- Healthier relationships
- Lower healthcare burden
- Greater civic engagement

7.18 Long-Term Benefits of Integrative Living

Living with awareness of 'I' and body alignment leads to:

- Lifelong wellness
- Purpose-driven living
- Inner peace and outer success
- Resilience during crises

7.19 Common Misconceptions and Clarifications

- "Body is everything": Neglects the higher purpose of life
- "Body is evil": Disrespects the vessel that enables living
- "Emotions are part of the body": Emotions are felt in the body but arise in 'I'

Correct understanding bridges these divides.

7.20 Summary

Human beings are co-existential entities composed of the conscious 'I' and the physical body. Recognizing their distinct roles and interdependence is crucial for holistic living. 'I' governs and guides, while the body executes and supports. Neglecting either results in imbalance and suffering. Through self-observation, reflection, and disciplined action, we can harmonize this duality and build a foundation for deeper understanding, ethical behavior, and lasting well-being. This chapter serves as the starting point for further exploration into the functions, activities, and harmonious integration of 'I' and the body in the upcoming chapters.

Chapter 8: Need Differentiation – Self vs. Body

NEED DIFFERENTIATION

SELF vs. BODY

Introduction

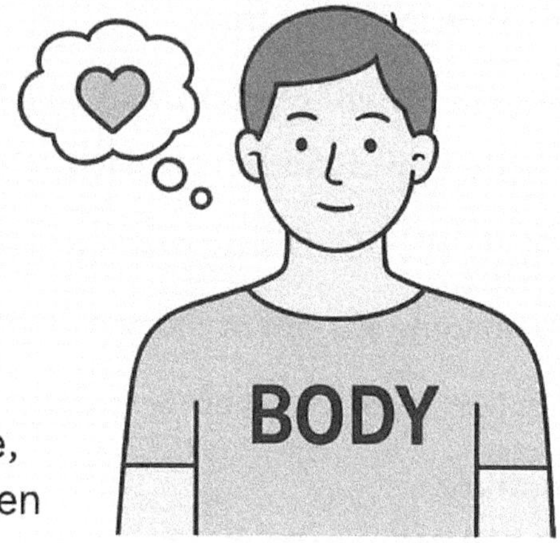

Human beings consist of "I" (the conscious self) and the body, each with distinct needs. The needs of 'I' are non-material, qualitative, and continuous, whereas the needs of the body are material, quantitative, and temporary. Differentiating between them is crucial for understanding and harmony.

Categories of Needs

Needs of 'I' (Self)		Needs of Body	
Happiness Trust Respect	Happiness Trust Respect	Food Water Shelter	Shelter
Nature		Tangible	
Mode of fulfillment		Physical facilities	
Continuity	Continuous	Temporary	Food, water

Misalignment of Needs

- Buying luxury items to gain respect
- Eating junk food to relieve sadneess
- Seeking entertainment to escape loneliness

Prioritizing Self Over Body

- Make value-based choices
- Exercise self-control

8.1 Introduction

The recognition of human duality—of being composed of 'I' (conscious self) and the body—forms the foundation for a deeper understanding of human needs. While the previous chapter outlined this dual existence, this chapter explores the distinctions between the needs of 'I' and those of the body. This distinction is fundamental to understanding how to live a life of balance, satisfaction, and harmony. Misunderstanding or confusing these needs often leads to inner conflict, stress, overconsumption, and dissatisfaction. By clearly identifying and fulfilling each need appropriately, we pave the way toward holistic well-being.

8.2 Why Distinguish Needs?

Most challenges in modern living stem from the overemphasis on bodily needs while neglecting the deeper needs of the self. This disproportion leads to:

- Pursuit of wealth without inner peace
- Physical comfort without contentment
- External achievements with internal emptiness

A balanced life requires meeting both categories of needs but with proper prioritization and clarity.

8.3 Categories of Human Needs

1. **Needs of the Self (I)**:
    - Non-material in nature
    - Qualitative, continuous, and non-accumulative
    - Fulfilled through right understanding and right feelings
    - Include: happiness, trust, respect, love, peace, knowledge
2. **Needs of the Body**:
    - Material in nature
    - Quantitative, temporary, and recurring
    - Fulfilled through physical facilities (food, clothing, shelter, medicine)

Comparison Table:

Aspect	Needs of 'I' (Self)	Needs of Body
Nature	Intangible	Tangible
Mode of Fulfillment	Right understanding & right feelings	Physical facilities
Continuity	Continuous (always needed)	Temporary (interval-based)

Examples	Happiness, respect, trust, knowledge	Food, water, clothing, rest
Mode of Satisfaction	Through relationships and clarity	Through material consumption
Development	Through education and reflection	Through hygiene, nutrition, fitness

8.4 Misalignment of Needs

In many life situations, individuals try to satisfy the needs of 'I' through material means:

- Buying luxury items to gain respect
- Eating junk food to relieve sadness
- Seeking entertainment to escape loneliness

Such misalignments provide only short-term relief and often result in:

- Psychological stress
- Health deterioration
- Relationship breakdowns

8.5 The Role of Happiness

Happiness is a state of **inner contentment**, **peace**, and **fulfillment**. It arises when:

- One lives in harmony with self and surroundings
- Desires, thoughts, and actions are aligned
- There is clarity about one's purpose

Happiness cannot be consumed, purchased, or accumulated. It is a **result of the quality of our understanding and relationships**.

8.6 Physical Needs: Importance and Limits

Bodily needs are genuine and essential, but limited:

- Food keeps the body energized
- Clothing protects against weather
- Shelter provides safety

Once fulfilled, any excess adds little value and can cause harm (e.g., overeating, overconsumption).

Balanced Approach:

- Meet physical needs adequately and sustainably

- Use physical resources as instruments for higher human goals

8.7 Prioritizing Self over Body

Although both 'I' and the body require care, the **self must lead**, and the **body must follow**. This means:

- Making choices rooted in values rather than impulses
- Exercising self-control and mindfulness
- Using the body to express right understanding (e.g., speech, actions)

Example: Choosing to speak respectfully (a decision by 'I') even when angry (a reaction felt in the body).

8.8 Common Confusions in Modern Life

Buying respect: Mistaking expensive clothes or gadgets as sources of respect

Food as comfort: Emotional eating replacing genuine emotional expression

Social media likes = love: Mistaking external validation for internal connection

These habits obscure the true sources of happiness and disconnect people from their values.

8.9 Practice Session: Identifying Needs of 'I' and Body

Activity 1: Personal Reflection Exercise

Make two columns.

In the left column, list what you needed yesterday.

In the right column, categorize each need as 'Self' or 'Body'.

Sample:

Need Experienced	Category
Food at lunch	**Body**
Appreciation from friend	**Self**
Sleep at night	**Body**
Clarity about decision	**Self**

Activity 2: Group Discussion

Share examples of when someone tried to fulfill a self-need with a body-based solution.

How effective was it?

Objective:
To help participants distinguish between needs and realize the importance of fulfilling them through appropriate means.

8.10 Internal Harmony Through Correct Fulfillment

When needs are rightly understood and addressed:

One feels more peaceful, clear, and joyful

Behavior aligns with values

Relationships become more authentic

Harmony is not the absence of needs—it is their proper identification and satisfaction.

8.11 Impact on Lifestyle Choices

Understanding the difference influences our:

- **Consumption patterns**: Simplicity and sustainability over luxury

- **Social behavior**: Empathy over competition
- **Health**: Balanced diet, exercise, and emotional hygiene
- **Education**: Focus on self-exploration along with academics

8.12 Implications for Society

A society that prioritizes body over self often witnesses:

- Consumerism and materialism
- Pollution and ecological damage
- Mental health issues

A value-based society nurtures:

- Minimalism
- Community wellness
- Ethical living

8.13 Educational Reforms for Need Clarity

Value education must:

- Teach need differentiation explicitly
- Encourage reflective practices
- Offer experiential learning (e.g., service, silence, nature walks)

Example: Assignments involving observing needs over a week and reflecting on them.

8.14 Case Studies: Need Misalignment and Realignment

Case 1: A student obsessed with exam scores neglects friendships and sleep. Eventually, she feels burned out and lonely. Value education helps her realign by prioritizing health, purpose, and genuine learning.

Case 2: A professional compensates emotional emptiness with frequent shopping. Realization of inner needs leads to engaging in meaningful relationships and volunteer work.

8.15 Role of Media and Culture

Modern advertising often blurs the lines between self and body needs:

- "Drink this to feel special"
- "Wear this to be respected"

Critical thinking and value discernment help protect against such manipulation.

8.16 Practice Session: 24-Hour Need Awareness Journal

- Record every need felt in a day.

- Categorize: Self or Body?
- Analyze the response: Was the method of fulfillment appropriate?

Follow-up Questions:

- What patterns did you notice?
- Where was there misalignment?
- What could you change tomorrow?

8.17 Long-Term Benefits of Differentiating Needs

- Increased emotional resilience
- Sustainable lifestyle habits
- Improved decision-making
- Greater life satisfaction

8.18 Philosophical and Cultural Insights

- **Indian philosophy** distinguishes 'Sharir' and 'Atma', emphasizing detachment and inner fulfillment.
- **Stoicism** in Western thought teaches mastery over desires.
- **Zen Buddhism** promotes minimalism and clarity in distinction.

These traditions reinforce the importance of right identification of human needs.

8.19 Educator's Role in Reinforcing Understanding

- Create activities that explore choices and consequences
- Promote open discussion on emotional needs
- Encourage creative expression (writing, art, music) of self-needs

8.20 Summary

Understanding the difference between the needs of 'I' and those of the body is foundational to value-based living. The self seeks understanding, love, and purpose, while the body requires care and nourishment. Fulfillment of self-needs through material means is a common but flawed approach that leads to dissatisfaction. Through reflection, education, and mindful living, we can align our actions with our real needs and lead lives that are joyful, responsible, and sustainable. The next chapter will examine how the body functions as an instrument of the self and how governance of the body by the self ensures well-being and ethical behavior.

Chapter 9: Body as an Instrument of 'I' – Governance & Decision-Making

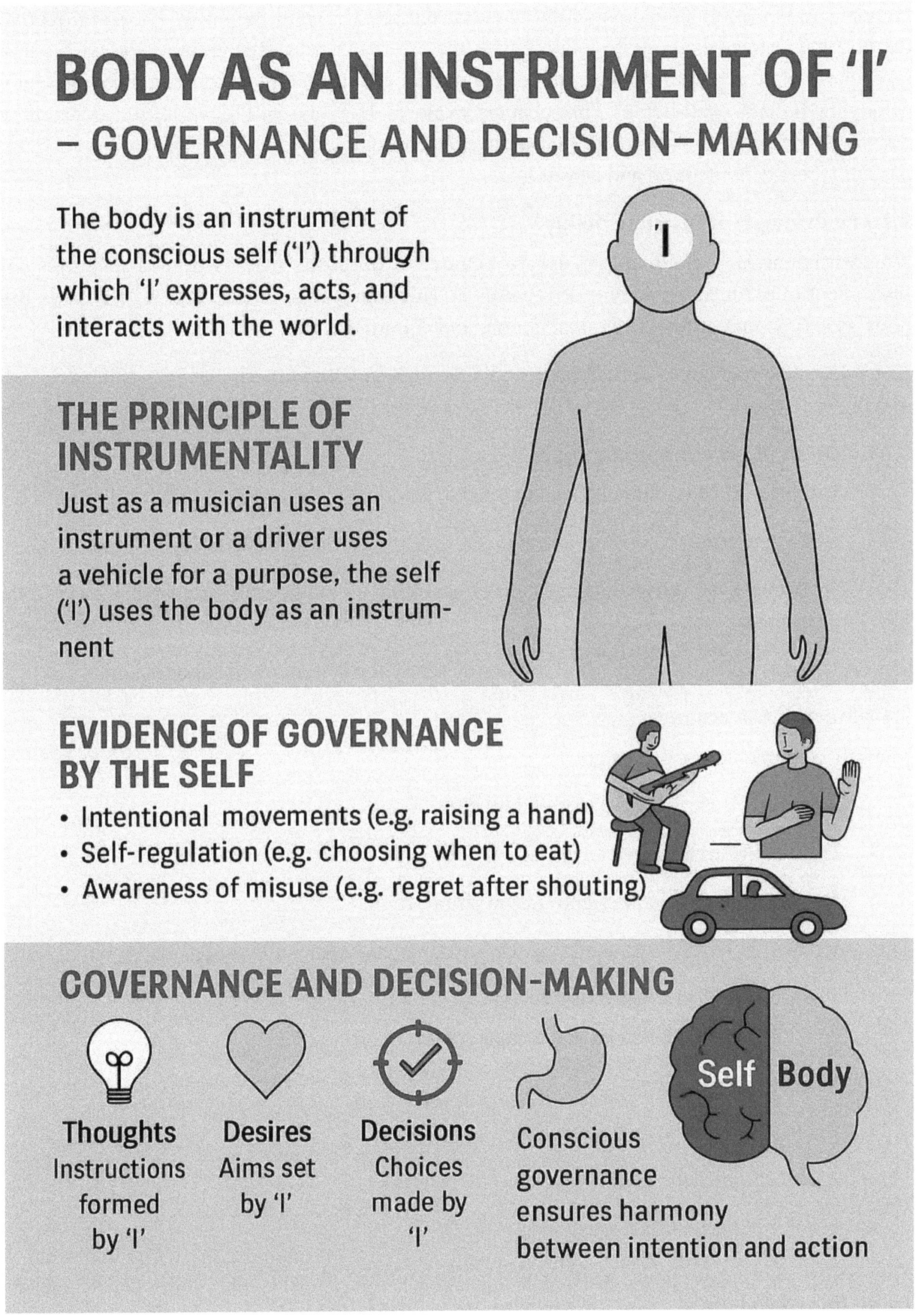

9.1 Introduction

Human life is a continuous interaction between the self ('I') and the body. The self governs, directs, and utilizes the body to interact with the external world. Recognizing the body as an instrument of 'I' is central to understanding human behavior, cultivating ethical conduct, and achieving holistic well-being. This chapter explores how the self governs the body, how decisions are made by the self, and what role conscious awareness plays in maintaining harmony between intention and action.

9.2 The Principle of Instrumentality

An instrument is something we use to achieve a purpose. Just as a musician uses an instrument to produce music or a driver uses a vehicle to travel, the human self ('I') uses the body as an instrument for expression, action, and communication.

Key Idea: The body does not act independently; it is governed by the self through decision-making processes.

9.3 Evidence of Governance by the Self

- **Intentional Movements**: Raising a hand, walking, speaking—all initiated by the self
- **Self-regulation**: Choosing when to eat, rest, or respond emotionally
- **Awareness of Misuse**: Regret after shouting or indulging indicates higher self-awareness

The body responds to the signals and intentions set by the self, even in habitual actions.

9.4 Nature of Governance

The self governs the body through:

- **Thoughts**: Instructions generated by the self
- **Desires**: Motivations or aims the self sets
- **Expectations**: Outcomes anticipated from actions

This inner process of desiring, thinking, and deciding constitutes internal governance.

9.5 Decision-Making as a Human Faculty

Unlike animals, human beings have the capacity to:

- Reflect before acting
- Evaluate long-term consequences
- Align actions with values
- Modify behavior consciously

This ability to choose consciously is what distinguishes human beings and places ethical responsibility on them.

9.6 Examples of Governance and Choice

- Deciding to skip a meal to help a friend
- Choosing silence over retaliation in an argument
- Delaying gratification for a greater good

Each of these choices shows the self's ability to override bodily impulses for higher values.

9.7 Factors Influencing Decision-Making

1. **Clarity of Understanding**: Right understanding enables ethical and sustainable decisions
2. **Emotional State**: Anger or fear can cloud judgment
3. **External Pressures**: Peer pressure, social expectations
4. **Value Framework**: Internalized ethics and beliefs

Balanced decisions arise from clarity in all four factors.

9.8 Alignment Between Self and Body

True well-being comes when:

- The self gives clear and right instructions
- The body executes them effectively
- There is no contradiction between intention and behavior

Example: Wanting to wake early (self) but staying in bed due to habit (body) indicates misalignment.

9.9 Misgovernance and Its Consequences

When the self fails to govern the body properly:

- Unhealthy habits form
- Emotions dominate actions
- Values are compromised

Common results:

- Addictions
- Aggression
- Regret and guilt

9.10 The Body's Role in Execution

While the self decides, the body:

- Enables movement and action

- Provides sensory feedback
- Displays psychosomatic symptoms (stress, joy)

It is a responsive and adaptable system but cannot decide autonomously.

9.11 Practice Session: Observing Governance in Daily Life

Activity 1: Reflective Logging

- Track decisions made in a day (e.g., food, words, responses)
- Note which were led by the self's clarity vs. bodily impulse

Activity 2: Thought-Awareness Dialogue

- Pause before reacting
- Ask: "Is this action aligned with my values or driven by impulse?"

Objective: Build real-time awareness of self-governance.

9.12 Role of Discipline and Training

Like an instrument needs tuning, the body needs discipline to function in harmony with the self:

- Regular sleep, exercise, and diet
- Avoidance of stimulants and distractions
- Mindfulness and mental rest

Self-care is not indulgence—it is responsible management.

9.13 Self as the Driver – Body as the Vehicle

In this analogy:

- 'I' is the driver with vision and direction
- The body is the vehicle with capacity and speed

Without conscious governance, the vehicle may crash or go in the wrong direction. But without the vehicle, the driver cannot reach anywhere.

9.14 Governance and Ethics

Ethical living depends on the self's governance:

- Choosing fairness over convenience
- Resisting immediate pleasure for long-term well-being
- Speaking truth despite discomfort

Conscious governance = Ethical conduct

9.15 Governance in Relationships

- Choosing to listen with empathy
- Responding with kindness in conflicts
- Apologizing when wrong despite ego

All these require the self to govern over emotional and physical impulses.

9.16 Influence of Conditioning on Governance

Our upbringing and culture shape our decisions. Sometimes:

- We act out of habit, not clarity
- We conform to norms, not truth

Practice: Question inherited assumptions. Ask: "Does this belief serve harmony and well-being?"

9.17 Health and Governance

When the self governs the body wisely:

- Health improves
- Stress decreases
- Immunity strengthens

When the body is neglected or misused:

- Lifestyle diseases develop
- Addictions form
- Emotional distress manifests physically

9.18 Education and Self-Governance

Education must:

- Empower self-awareness
- Promote emotional regulation
- Encourage self-directed learning
- Foster decision-making aligned with universal values

9.19 Case Study: Realignment of Governance

Case: Rohit, a student, feels tired and irritable. He binge eats, skips classes, and procrastinates. After attending a self-exploration workshop, he realizes:

- His 'I' was misaligned with bodily habits
- He lacked discipline and clarity

He restructures his day, builds mindfulness routines, and experiences renewed energy and purpose.

9.20 Summary

The body is not the controller—it is the medium. 'I' is the conscious center of decision-making and governance. Recognizing this relationship is vital for ethical behavior, emotional regulation, physical health, and inner peace. Governance is not control through fear but alignment through understanding. The more consciously the self governs the body, the more meaningful and harmonious life becomes. In the following chapters, we will explore the detailed activities and characteristics of the self to deepen this understanding and strengthen inner clarity.

Chapter 10
Activities and Characteristics of 'I' – Desire, Thought, and Expectation

Introduction

- 'I' is the conscious entity that
- Reflects
- Understands
- Desires
- Active eveen when the Body is at rest
- It is intangible, but observable through introspection and behavior

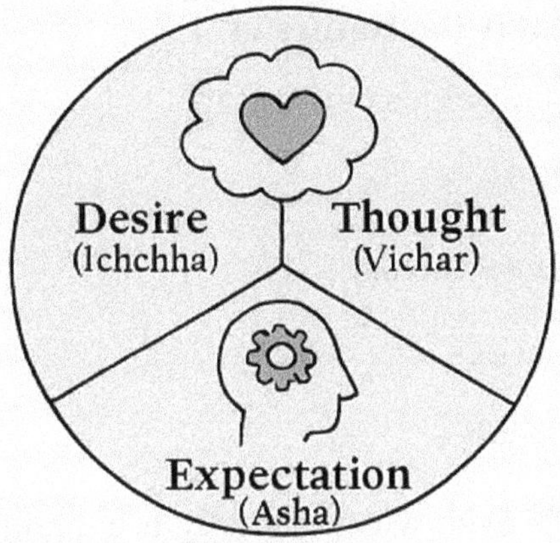

Primary Activities of 'I'

1 **Desire** (Ichchha)
   – The intention or want for something

2 **Thought** (Vichar)
   – The process of exploring, analyzing, evaluating

3 **Expectation** (Asha)
   – Assessment er anticipation of outcomes

Cycle Example:
Desire: I want respect →
Thought: How can I gain it?
→ **Expectation:** If I speak kindly and contribute, I'll be respected

Interconnection of the Three Activities

These activities form a dynamic cycle

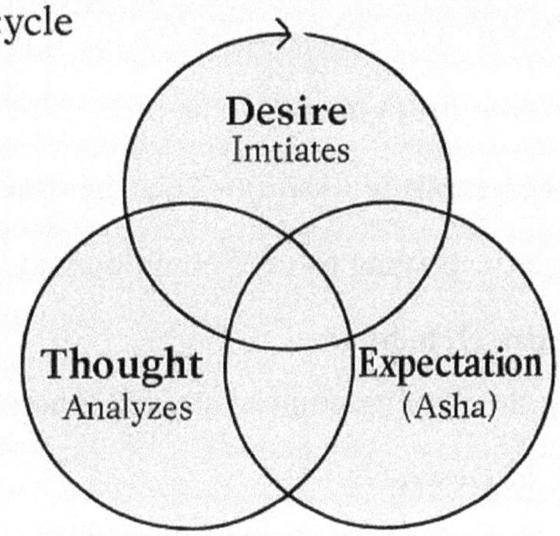

Expection: shapes myucee?

Practice Session: Mapping Inner Activity

Activity 1: Inner Event Reflection

- Recall a recent decision
- identify your desire, thouought process, and expectation
- Reflect: Were they harmonious?

Activity 2: Dally Rection Table

Time	Desire Felt	Expectation

10.1 Introduction

After understanding the governance relationship between the self ('I') and the body, it becomes essential to delve deeper into the workings of 'I' itself. This chapter focuses on three core activities of 'I': Desire (Ichchha), Thought (Vichar), and Expectation (Asha). By observing and analyzing these functions, we begin to uncover how the self engages with the world and how these activities shape our emotions, decisions, relationships, and behavior. Understanding and harmonizing these activities leads to inner peace, clear purpose, and balanced living.

10.2 What is the Nature of 'I'?

'I' is the conscious entity that:

- Reflects
- Understands
- Desires
- Decides

It is active even when the body is at rest (e.g., during sleep or deep thinking). 'I' is intangible, but its activities are observable through introspection and behavior.

10.3 Primary Activities of 'I'

'I' continuously engages in three fundamental and interlinked activities:

1. **Desire (Ichchha)** – The intention or want for something
2. **Thought (Vichar)** – The process of exploring, analyzing, and evaluating
3. **Expectation (Asha)** – The assessment or anticipation of outcomes

These are the driving forces behind human consciousness and behavior.

10.4 Desire (Ichchha)

Desire is the starting point of any inner activity. It reflects what we aim for, pursue, or value.

Sources of Desire:

- Sensory experiences
- Past memories
- Social conditioning
- Self-reflection

Types of Desires:

- Genuine: Rooted in understanding (e.g., to learn, to contribute)
- Conditioned: Borrowed from others without reflection (e.g., to impress, to possess)

Question: Are your desires your own, or are they borrowed?

10.5 Thought (Vichar)

Thought is the analytical process used to evaluate desires.

- Is this desire meaningful?
- How can I fulfill it?
- What are its implications?

Through thought, we gain clarity and devise action paths. Thoughts shape our worldview and choices.

Unclear thoughts lead to:

- Confusion
- Indecisiveness
- Misjudgments

10.6 Expectation (Asha)

Expectation is our projection of the results we seek or believe will occur.

- How will people react?
- What will I achieve?
- Will this bring happiness?

It reflects our value system and vision for fulfillment.

Right expectations align with:

- Universal human values
- Long-term well-being
- Realistic understanding

10.7 Interconnection of the Three Activities

These activities form a dynamic cycle:

- Desire initiates the process
- Thought analyzes and plans
- Expectation shapes motivation and behavior

Cycle Example:

- Desire: I want respect
- Thought: How can I gain it?

- Expectation: If I speak kindly and contribute, I'll be respected

10.8 Observation of Inner Processes

Through self-observation, we can:

- Identify habitual desires
- Understand thought patterns
- Assess expectations for alignment with values

Practice: Daily journaling of these activities to build inner clarity.

10.9 Desire Clarity and Human Fulfillment

Desires determine the direction of our life. When they are:

- **Unexamined**: We chase illusions
- **Misguided**: We feel unfulfilled even after achieving goals
- **Conflicted**: We feel divided and anxious

Clarity in desire is the first step to happiness.

10.10 Thought as the Instrument of Understanding

Thought serves as the self's tool for:

- Learning
- Decision-making
- Creative problem-solving

When directed by clear desires and values, thoughts become constructive. When governed by confusion or fear, they become reactive.

10.11 Expectation and Emotional Regulation

Expectations influence emotions. Misaligned expectations often lead to:

- Disappointment
- Resentment
- Anxiety

Realistic and value-based expectations bring resilience and satisfaction.

10.12 Impact of Unharmony in Desire-Thought-Expectation

When these activities are not in sync:

- We feel conflicted (e.g., want something, but think it's wrong)
- We act impulsively without considering consequences

- We suffer from emotional turmoil

10.13 Practice Session: Mapping Inner Activity

Activity 1: Inner Event Reflection

- Recall a recent decision
- Identify your desire, thought process, and expectation
- Reflect: Were they harmonious? Did the outcome bring peace?

Activity 2: Daily Reflection Table

Time Desire Felt Thought Process Expectation Harmony Rating (1-5)

10.14 Re-educating the Self

Many desires and expectations stem from social conditioning. We need to:

- Question inherited beliefs
- Explore personal meaning
- Rebuild desires aligned with values like trust, love, and purpose

10.15 Cultivating Conscious Living

Conscious living means:

- Knowing why we want what we want
- Thinking before reacting
- Evaluating expectations without assumptions

Tools for Conscious Living:

- Meditation
- Dialogue
- Reflective reading
- Mentorship

10.16 Alignment with Natural Acceptance

Natural acceptance helps:

- Evaluate whether desires are authentic
- Align thoughts with universal harmony
- Set expectations that are humanly enriching

Example:

Natural acceptance tells us respect is preferable to fear, truth to deceit.

10.17 Case Studies in Inner Activity Awareness

Case 1: A student chooses a career to please parents, but internally desires creative work. Misalignment causes stress. Through reflection, they find a path that honors both values.

Case 2: A manager reacts angrily to criticism. Upon reflection, she finds her desire for perfection led to unrealistic expectations. Awareness transforms her response style.

10.18 Role of Education in Inner Clarity

Educational institutions should:

- Facilitate introspection sessions
- Use storytelling and dialogue
- Provide safe spaces for self-expression
- Emphasize purpose-driven learning

10.19 Benefits of Harmonizing D-T-E

- Inner peace
- Ethical conduct
- Emotional intelligence
- Purposeful relationships
- Fulfillment beyond material success

10.20 Summary

Desire, thought, and expectation are the foundational activities of 'I'. These processes shape our intentions, decisions, and emotions. Understanding and harmonizing them leads to inner clarity, ethical action, and joyful living. When these activities reflect our natural acceptance and universal human values, we feel aligned and purposeful. In the following chapters, we explore how to maintain this alignment through the practice of Sanyam (self-regulation) and achieve holistic health and prosperity.

Chapter 11: Sanyam and Health – The Inner-Outer Harmony

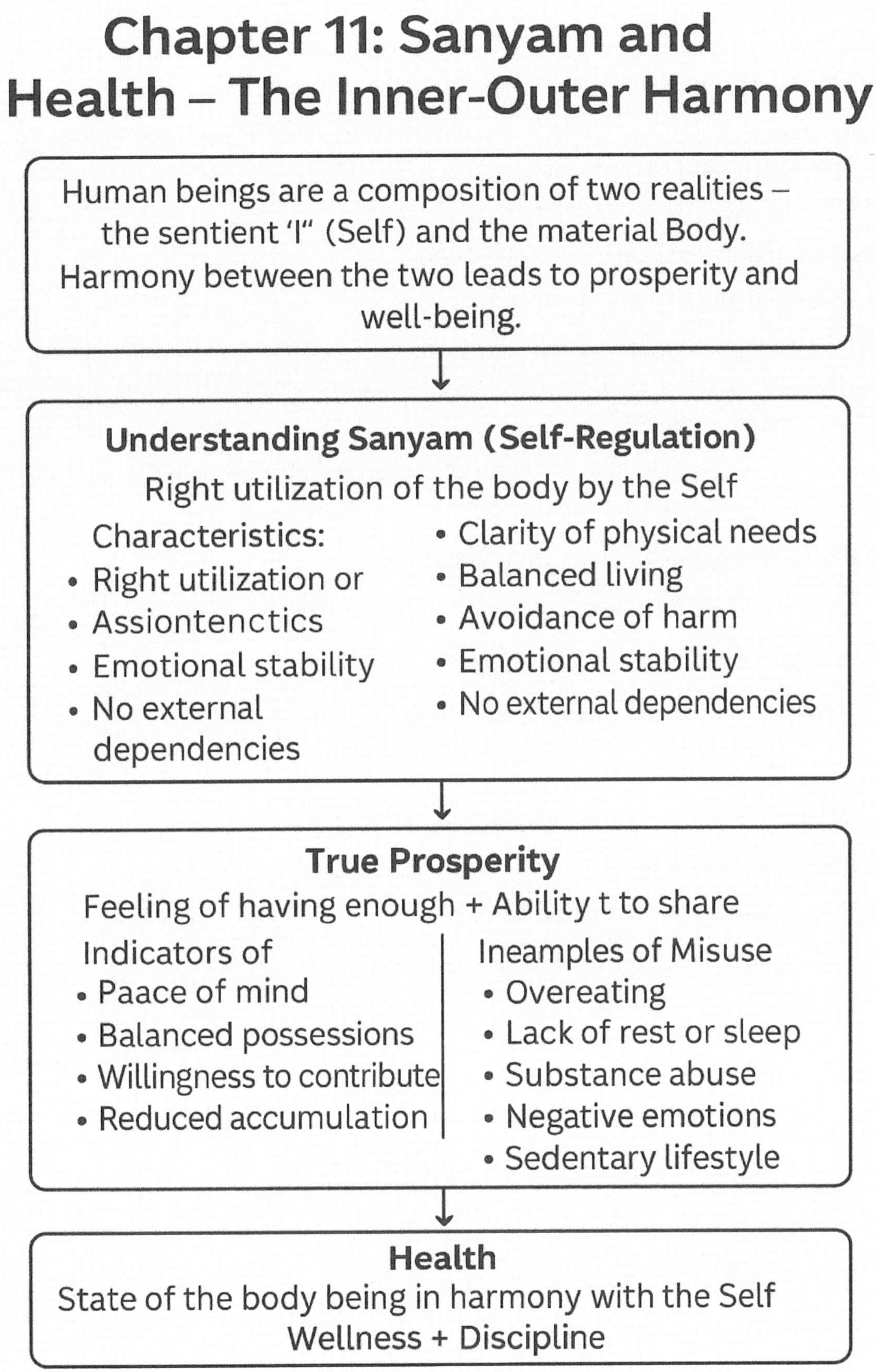

11.1 Introduction: Integrating the Inner and the Outer

Human beings are a unique composition of two realities: the sentient 'I' (the Self) and the material 'Body.' A meaningful life arises when there is harmony between these two. In this chapter, we explore the concepts of **Sanyam** (self-regulation) and **Health**, not as external impositions but as natural outcomes of right understanding and right living.

Harmony between the 'I' and the Body manifests in the form of regulated desires, balanced habits, appropriate physical needs, and mental peace. This leads to *prosperity* and *well-being* — not merely in material terms, but as a deeply human experience.

11.2 Understanding Sanyam (Self-Regulation)

11.2.1 Definition and Essence of Sanyam

Sanyam means *right utilization* of the body by the Self. It is the state in which the Self (I) has clarity about the needs of the Body, governs its activities appropriately, and ensures there is no overuse, misuse, or abuse.

Sanyam is *not suppression*, but the **natural expression of responsibility** guided by right understanding. It emerges from within, not by force or fear.

11.2.2 Characteristics of a Person with Sanyam

- Clarity of physical needs
- Balanced food, sleep, work, and recreation
- Avoidance of harmful substances and habits
- Emotional stability
- No dependency on external indulgences for happiness

11.3 Redefining Prosperity

11.3.1 Conventional View of Prosperity

In the current paradigm, prosperity is associated with:

- High income
- Ownership of assets
- Accumulation of luxury goods
- Social prestige through material abundance

However, this view leads to:

- Overexploitation of resources
- Competition and stress
- Never-ending dissatisfaction

11.3.2 True Prosperity

Prosperity = Feeling of having enough + Ability to share.

In the context of Universal Human Values:

- It is not about having more and more.
- It is about knowing how much is enough.
- It involves correct appraisal of physical needs.
- It is about mutual fulfillment, not individual hoarding.

A prosperous person is not the one who has more, but the one who knows *he has enough* and is willing to share.

11.3.3 Indicators of True Prosperity

- Peace of mind
- Balanced material possessions
- Willingness to contribute
- Reduced desire for accumulation
- Freedom from greed and insecurity

11.4 Understanding Health: A Function of Sanyam

11.4.1 What is Health?

Health is the state of the body being in harmony with the Self. It is not just the absence of disease, but a positive state of well-being.

Health involves:

- Proper functioning of bodily systems
- Energetic and alert state
- Mental calmness
- Clarity of purpose and direction

11.4.2 Health = Wellness + Discipline

- **Wellness** refers to a balanced state of the body in its functioning and energy.
- **Discipline** arises from Sanyam. It means fulfilling bodily needs rightly — food, rest, cleanliness, exercise, etc.

Health is a result of a Self that takes care of the Body with awareness, not negligence or indulgence.

11.5 The Interconnectedness of Prosperity, Sanyam, and Health

Aspect	False View	Right Understanding
Prosperity	More accumulation = More security	Enough + Sharing = True security
Sanyam	Self-control by suppression	Self-regulation through clarity and awareness
Health	Body managed by external means	Body nurtured through right usage by 'I'

Health is sustained when:

- Sanyam is practiced,
- Needs are correctly understood,
- The body is treated as an instrument,
- Excesses are avoided,
- Harmony with surroundings is maintained.

11.6 The Misuse of the Body and Its Consequences

Misuse	Consequences
Overeating	Obesity, fatigue, diseases
Lack of rest/sleep	Poor immunity, mental fog
Substance abuse	Addiction, organ failure
Negative emotions (anger, envy)	Stress, anxiety, depression
Sedentary lifestyle	Metabolic disorders, stiffness

Without Sanyam, misuse becomes common. The body is exploited for temporary pleasure, often resulting in suffering and disease.

11.7 Practice Session: How Others Contribute to My Material Well-being

Objective:

To help learners recognize their interconnectedness with others and develop gratitude toward society.

Activity: Reflective Exercise

Step 1: Choose three items you used today (e.g., a pencil, your shirt, a mobile phone).

Step 2: Trace their origins:

- Who made them?
- Who transported them?

- Who helped you acquire them?

Step 3: Reflect on:

- The number of people involved
- The interdependence of roles
- The invisible support system around you

Learning Outcome:

- Realize the vast network of people involved in your daily comfort.
- Understand the *dependence on others* for physical needs.
- Develop **gratitude** and **a sense of responsibility**.
- Recognize the **need to use resources wisely and compassionately**.

11.8 Real-life Applications of Sanyam and Health

In Food Choices

- Eating when hungry, not out of boredom
- Preferring natural, unprocessed food
- Avoiding overeating

In Sleep Patterns

- Sleeping as per body's requirement
- Not forcing wakefulness or oversleeping

In Technology Use

- Using gadgets with purpose
- Avoiding overuse that leads to stress or isolation

In Emotions

- Observing feelings
- Avoiding impulsive reactions
- Practicing forgiveness and empathy

11.9 Case Studies

Case Study 1: Sanyam in the Life of a Student

Ravi is a college student with constant headaches and poor focus. Through value education, he learns to regulate his diet, sleep, and gadget usage. Within a month, his health improves, and he feels calmer and more productive.

Case Study 2: A Family's Journey to True Prosperity

The Gupta family earns well but constantly worries about money. After attending a workshop, they re-evaluate their expenses and redefine "needs." They cut down wasteful spending, donate to a shelter, and report feeling *more abundant than ever*.

11.10 Summary of Key Points

- **Sanyam** is the basis for right living.
- **Prosperity** is a feeling of having enough with the capacity to share.
- **Health** is a dynamic harmony between the 'I' and the Body.
- Misuse of the body without Sanyam leads to imbalance and disease.
- Acknowledging how others contribute to our well-being fosters **gratitude** and **humility**.
- Right understanding simplifies life, bringing joy, peace, and energy.

11.11 Reflection Questions

1. Do I know what my body truly needs, and do I meet it consciously?
2. Have I ever misused my body? What were the results?
3. Can I recall instances where others contributed to my physical comfort without me noticing?
4. What does "enough" mean to me?
5. How can I bring more Sanyam into my daily routine?

Chapter 12: Ensuring Health vs. Managing Disease

Living in Harmony Through Self-Regulation and Awareness

CHAPTER 12

ENSURING HEALTH vs. MANAGING DISEASE

Living in Harmony Through Self-Regulation ad Awareness

INTRODUCTION: THE BROADER MEANING OF HEALTH

Modern misinterpretions of health as just the absence of disease - conviring physical, mental, emotional, social, and spiritual dimensions- ainal dimensions.

UNDERSTANDING HEALTH AND DISEASE

WHAT IS HEALTH?

Dimersion	Explanation
Physlological	A stable and calm inner state, free of excessive stress or anxiety
Mental & Emotional	Harmonious relationships with others
Social	A sense of purpose, gratitude, and inner fulfillment

WHAT IS DISEASE?

Disease as a deviation from natural harmony.

- Physical imbalance
- Mental or emotional distress
- Social disharmony

WHAT IS DISEASE?

Rependsa a deviation from natural harmony.

✓ Reactive, curative

ENSURING HEALTH vs. MANAGING DISEASE

Aspect	Preventive,	Managing Disease
Approach	Preventive, proactive,	Reactive, curative symptom-focused
Focus	Overall harmony and well-being	Elimination of specific symptoms or condition

Modern medicine plays a valuable role-in emergencies and acute conditions, However, lasting health ean only emerge from conscious living, driven by clanty, harmony, and responsibility.

12.1 Introduction: The Broader Meaning of Health

In today's fast-paced, technology-driven lifestyle, health is often misinterpreted as merely the absence of disease. But **true health** is a much deeper, **holistic state** — encompassing physical, mental, emotional, social, and spiritual dimensions.

This chapter explores the **difference between ensuring health** (proactive well-being) and **managing disease** (reactive treatment). We also highlight the role of **Sanyam (self-regulation)** as the cornerstone of lasting wellness, and offer **practical assessment tools** for evaluating and improving one's lifestyle.

12.2 Understanding Health and Disease

12.2.1 What is Health?

Health is a state of **well-being at all levels** of human existence. It is more than just a functioning body — it's about harmony:

Dimension	Explanation
Physiological	All body systems (respiratory, digestive, circulatory, etc.) functioning properly
Mental & Emotional	A stable and calm inner state, free of excessive stress or anxiety
Social	Harmonious relationships with others
Spiritual	A sense of purpose, gratitude, and inner fulfillment

When these levels are aligned and nurtured, **health arises naturally** as a state of equilibrium.

12.2.2 What is Disease?

Disease is a **deviation from this natural harmony**. It represents:

- **Physical imbalance**, such as malfunctioning organs or systems
- **Mental or emotional distress**, like anxiety, frustration, or depression
- **Social disharmony**, including conflict or isolation

Disease often results from:

- Improper lifestyle choices
- Misuse or neglect of the body
- Lack of self-awareness or Sanyam
- Environmental stressors (pollution, noise, etc.)

12.3 Ensuring Health vs. Managing Disease

Let's differentiate these two fundamentally distinct approaches:

Aspect	**Ensuring Health**	**Managing Disease**
Approach	Preventive, proactive, holistic	Reactive, curative, symptom-focused
Focus	Overall harmony and well-being	Elimination of specific symptoms or conditions
Responsibility	Primarily individual (self-awareness and regulation)	Shared with doctors, hospitals, external systems
Methods	Balanced lifestyle, self-discipline, right understanding	Medicines, surgeries, therapies
Result	Sustainable health, inner balance	Temporary relief, possible side effects

Insight:

Modern medicine plays a valuable role in emergencies and acute conditions. However, **lasting health can only emerge from conscious living**, driven by clarity, harmony, and responsibility.

12.4 The Role of Sanyam (Self-Regulation)

Sanyam is the **key enabler** of health. It refers to the ability of the *Self* (I) to:

- **Understand** the needs of the body
- **Respond appropriately**, avoiding indulgence or negligence
- **Maintain awareness** over desires, actions, and outcomes

12.4.1 Aspects of Sanyam in Health

Area	**Self-Regulated Practice**
Diet	Eating only when hungry, preferring fresh and balanced food
Physical Activity	Daily movement, yoga, or exercise suited to the body's condition
Sleep	Consistent and adequate rest without external disturbance
Emotions	Awareness and resolution of stress, anger, fear
Social Behavior	Honest, caring relationships without domination or dependence

When **Sanyam** becomes a way of life, it **naturally prevents disease** and fosters harmony — within and without.

12.5 Practice Session: Lifestyle Audit + Health Checklist

These tools encourage **self-reflection** and **personal responsibility**, essential for maintaining health.

A. Lifestyle Audit

Reflect on your daily habits. Mark each with ✅ (Yes) or ❌ (No):

Habit	✅/❌
I eat only when I'm hungry	
I consume fresh, home-cooked meals	
I exercise or move my body regularly	
I sleep and wake up at regular times	
I avoid unnecessary screen time	
I spend time with family or loved ones	
I take time to reflect or meditate daily	
I avoid intoxicants or harmful substances	
I manage anger and stress consciously	
I express gratitude and positivity daily	

Scoring:

- ✅ 8–10: Healthy, balanced lifestyle
- ✅ 5–7: Moderately balanced – some changes needed
- ✅<5: High risk – immediate attention recommended

B. Personal Health Checklist

Rate yourself on a scale of 1 (Poor) to 5 (Excellent):

Aspect	Rating (1–5)
Physical energy levels	
Quality of sleep	
Emotional stability	

Ability to focus/concentrate	
Regularity in physical activity	
Digestive health	
Satisfaction with relationships	
Stress levels	
Spiritual or inner peace	
Overall sense of well-being	

Interpretation:

- **Score ≥ 40**: Excellent state of health and balance
- **Score 30–39**: Generally good; room for focused improvements
- **Score < 30**: Misalignment — consider making lifestyle adjustments

12.6 Health as a Natural Outcome of Harmony

Health is not something to "achieve"; it is the **natural consequence** of:

- Right understanding
- Balanced priorities
- Harmonious living
- Social and ecological awareness

When we live by **natural acceptance**, make informed choices, and act with **Sanyam**, the body responds positively. Disease becomes less frequent and less severe.

12.7 Disease as a Signal, Not an Enemy

Diseases are **messages from the body**. They signal:

- Overuse or misuse of the body
- Internal emotional conflicts
- Stress or unprocessed trauma
- Poor dietary/sleep routines

The goal is not merely to suppress the symptoms, but to understand the cause, change the lifestyle, and **restore internal balance**.

12.8 Institutional and Societal Support for Health

While individual responsibility is essential, institutions must create an ecosystem where health is nurtured:

Context	Health-Supportive Practices
Colleges	Mandatory yoga/meditation, healthy meals, mental wellness sessions
Workplaces	Breaks for movement, ergonomic setups, stress counseling
Governments	Clean environment policies, public health education

12.9 Summary of Key Learnings

- **Health** is a state of complete harmony at all levels: body, mind, relationships, and spirit.
- **Disease** is a result of imbalance or misalignment in thought, behavior, or environment.
- **Ensuring health** is a proactive process — grounded in lifestyle, self-awareness, and responsibility.
- **Sanyam** is the key to long-term wellness — enabling clarity, moderation, and correct appraisal of needs.
- Tools like the **Lifestyle Audit** and **Health Checklist** help track and realign our daily behavior.
- A supportive environment, both personal and societal, enhances our ability to live in health and harmony.

12.10 Reflection Questions

1. What does health mean to me — just absence of disease or something more?
2. How aligned is my current lifestyle with the principles of Sanyam?
3. Which habit (if improved) would significantly boost my well-being?
4. How does my social and work environment support (or harm) my health?
5. How can I inspire others in my family or workplace to adopt a more balanced lifestyle?

Chapter 13
Justice and Human Relationschips

13.1 Introduction: Why Relationships Matter

We all live in a web of relationships-with. family, friends, neighbors, and society. These connections are important for our happiness and sense of justice.

This chapter will help you.

- Learn about nine important values for good relationships
- Understand the importance of trust and respect
- Refiect on yourown relationships

13.2 Justice as Mutual Fulfilme-

Justice in relationships is not about courts ŏr rules erd means both peepie feel seen, respected, and happy.

Justice = Recognizing Other + Fulfilment = Mutual Happiness

True justice happens when:

- Both miiersta nd each other
- Both people care about other well-being

13.4 Understanding Trust: The Root of All Relationships

What is Trust?

Respest believe the other person wants you to be happy and will not hurt you on purpose.

Every person want: to lie happily and can do so

How to Show Respect

- Listen without interrupting

13.3 The Nine Universal Values in Human Relationships

There are nine values that help us build strong relationships:

These values w wrk ât four:

1. **Intention** (Inside us)

   Trust: Believing the other person wants good for you
2. **Thought**

   Respect: Seeing walmth ả nindness
   Affection: Feeling warmth
   Care: Wanting the other person
3. **Behavior**

   Guidance: Helping other person grow
   Reverence: Adminng good qualitien others
   Glory: Appreciating achievements
4. **Outcome** (Happiness)

   Gratitude: Thanking and appreciating others

13.5 Understanding Respect: Seeing the Other as They Are

What is Respect?

Respect means seeing the #ue invery person, not based on their money, status, or looks.

Every person wants to live happily and can do so.

Trust »Trust	Differentiation
Intention Thinks well of others	Based on status) Double and suspects others
Honest and open	Exclusion
Acceptance	Envy or superiority/ inferiority

13.1 Introduction: Why Relationships Matter

We all live in a web of relationships-with family, friends, neighbors, and society. These connections are important for our happiness and sense of justice.

This chapter will help you:

- Learn about nine important values for good relationships
- Understand the importance of trust and respect
- Reflect on your own relationships

13.2 Justice as Mutual Fulfillment

Justice in relationships is not about courts or rules. It means both people feel seen, respected, and happy.

Justice = Recognizing the other + Fulfillment = Mutual Happiness

True justice happens when:

- We understand each other
- Both people care about each other's well-being

13.3 The Nine Universal Values in Human Relationships

There are nine values that help us build strong relationships. These values work at four levels:

1. Intention (Inside us)

- **Trust**: Believing the other person wants good for you

2. Thought

- **Respect**: Seeing the value in the other person
- **Affection**: Feeling warmth and kindness
- **Care**: Wanting the other person to be well

3. Behavior

- **Guidance**: Helping the other person grow
- **Reverence**: Admiring good qualities in others
- **Glory**: Appreciating achievements

4. Outcome (Happiness)

- **Gratitude**: Thanking and appreciating others
- **Love**: Deep feeling of care and connection

These values show up in how we talk, help each other, and solve problems.

13.4 Understanding Trust: The Root of All Relationships

What is Trust?

- Trust means believing that the other person wants you to be happy and will not hurt you on purpose.
- Trust is about intention, not always about ability.

Trust vs. Mistrust Table

Aspect	Trust	Mistrust
Intention	Thinks well of others	Doubts and suspects others
Behavior	Honest and open	Defensive or aggressive
Consequence	Builds strong relationships	Causes fear and loneliness

How to Build Trust

- Question your own assumptions
- Talk openly instead of judging
- Avoid saying "They always do this"
- Be patient and try to understand

13.5 Understanding Respect: Seeing the Other as They Are

What is Respect?

- Respect means seeing the value in every person, not based on their money, status, or looks.
- Every person wants to live happily and can do so.

Respect vs. Differentiation Table

Basis of Value	Respect (All are equal)	Differentiation (Based on status)
Outcome	Inclusion	Exclusion
Feeling	Acceptance	Envy or superiority/inferiority

How to Show Respect

- Listen without interrupting
- Value other opinions, even if you disagree
- Avoid mocking or labeling
- Appreciate differences

13.6 A Framework for Evaluating Relationships

Ask yourself these questions about your relationships:

- Do I trust this person's intention?
- Do I respect them?
- Is there affection and care?
- Do we communicate openly?
- Do I show gratitude?
- Are both of us happy in this relationship?

13.7 Real-Life Scenarios: Applying the Nine Values

Conflict with a Friend

- Misunderstandings can break trust
- Solution: Talk openly, clarify intentions, rebuild trust, and show respect

Miscommunication with Parents

- You may feel controlled; they may feel unappreciated
- Solution: Be thankful, share your feelings respectfully, and show care

13.8 Practice Session: Reflect on Your Relationships

Activity Steps:

1. Pick a relationship that matters to you
2. Think about:
    - Do you trust this person?
    - Do you show them respect?
    - Is there affection and care?
    - Do you support each other?
3. Write a short note about:
    - How the relationship is now
    - Which values are present or missing
    - What you can do to improve it
4. (Optional) Share your thoughts with a group

Facilitator Tips

- Encourage honest sharing

- Focus on reflection, not judgment
- Make it a safe space

13.9 Transforming Relationships through Values

If you practice these values, you will notice:

- **Trust**: More openness
- **Respect**: Better communication, fewer fights
- **Affection**: Feeling safer emotionally
- **Gratitude**: More appreciation
- **Guidance**: Learning and growing together

13.10 Summary of Key Learnings

- Justice in relationships means both people feel seen and fulfilled
- Nine values help build strong relationships
- Trust and respect are the foundation
- Misunderstandings often come from wrong assumptions-talk about them
- Reflecting helps you see which values are present or missing
- With effort, any relationship can improve

13.11 Reflection Questions

1. Do I believe others want good for me?
2. How do I react if I feel disrespected?
3. Which value do I show most? Which is missing?
4. What would change if I showed more gratitude?
5. Can I remember a time when understanding helped a relationship?

UNDERSTANDING TRUST–
INTENTION AND COMPETENCE
THE FOUNDATION OF HEALTHY RELATIONSHIPS
Trust is truly believing soméone wánts good for you
TWO COMPONENTS
INTENTION
inner wish to do good
TWO COMPONENTS
INTENTION
inner wish to do good
Alex triéd tó ake a cake, but it didn't turn out well
COMPETENCE
skill / ability
Alex tried to bake a cake, but it didn't turn out well
HOW TO BUILD TRUST
Mistakes seen as bad intentions
REAL-LIFE EXAMPLES
communication
forgiveness
PRACTICE ACTIVITIES
Friénds
Family
School

14.1 Introduction: The Importance of Trust

Trust is the foundation of every healthy relationship. Whether it is with your family, friends, teachers, or anyone else, trust helps people feel safe, comfortable, and open with each other. Without trust, it is hard to share your thoughts and feelings. People may feel worried, scared, or alone when trust is missing.

When there is trust, relationships become strong and joyful. People can work together, help each other, and solve problems easily. Trust makes it possible to forgive mistakes, learn together, and grow as better human beings. That is why trust is the most basic and important value in any relationship.

14.2 What Does Trust Really Mean?

Trust means believing that the other person wants good for you. It means you feel sure that they will not hurt you on purpose. Trust is not just about believing blindly. It comes from understanding and seeing how the other person behaves over time.

When you trust someone, you feel relaxed around them. You can share your secrets, ask for help, and be yourself. Trust also means that you are willing to give the other person a chance, even if they make mistakes sometimes.

Trust is not something that happens overnight. It grows slowly as you get to know someone better. The more you see that someone cares about you, the more you trust them. In the same way, when you show care and honesty, others will trust you more.

14.3 The Two Sides of Trust: Intention and Competence

Many people think trust is only about whether someone keeps their promises or not. But trust is actually made up of two parts: **intention** and **competence**.

Intention

Intention is about what a person wants to do. It is their inner wish or purpose. When someone has a good intention, it means they want to do good for you. They want to help, support, or make you happy. Even if they do not always succeed, their wish is to do good.

Competence

Competence means having the skill or ability to do something well. Sometimes, a person wants to help you, but they do not know how. Or they try to do something good, but they make a mistake. This is not because they have a bad intention, but because they lack competence in that area.

Example

Imagine your friend wants to make you a birthday cake. They really want you to be happy (good intention), but they have never baked a cake before. The cake does not turn out well because they do not have the skill yet (low competence). Their intention was good, but their competence was not enough.

14.4 Why Do We Get Confused?

Many problems in relationships happen because people mix up intention and competence. When someone makes a mistake, we often think they did it on purpose, even if they just lacked the skill or knowledge. This can lead to fights, hurt feelings, and broken trust.

We also judge ourselves and others differently. When we make a mistake, we say, "I meant well, but I just didn't know how." But when someone else makes a mistake, we sometimes think, "They did not care enough," or "They did it on purpose." This is unfair and causes misunderstandings.

If we learn to see the difference between intention and competence, we can avoid many problems. We can forgive mistakes more easily and help each other improve.

14.5 How to Build and Maintain Trust

Building trust takes time and effort. Here are some simple ways to build and keep trust in your relationships:

1. Look for Good Intentions - Try to see the good in others. Before getting angry, ask yourself if the person meant to hurt you or if it was just a mistake. Most people want to do good, even if they are not always perfect.

2. Communicate Openly - If you feel hurt or confused, talk to the other person calmly. Share your feelings and ask about their intention. Open communication helps clear up misunderstandings.

3. Be Honest and Reliable - Be someone others can trust. Tell the truth, keep your promises, and admit your mistakes. When you are honest, people know they can count on you.

4. Forgive Mistakes - Everyone makes mistakes. If someone's intention was good, try to forgive them. Help them learn and improve their skills, instead of holding a grudge.

5. Support Each Other - Help each other grow. If someone lacks a skill, offer to teach or support them. When you help others, trust grows stronger.

14.6 Real-Life Situations: Understanding Trust

Situation 1: Family

Suppose your parent wants to help you with your homework. They try their best, but do not know the subject well. You might feel frustrated if they cannot help, but remember their intention is to support you, even if their competence is low.

Situation 2: Friends

Imagine your friend forgets your birthday. You feel hurt and think they do not care. But maybe they were busy or simply forgot. Their intention may still be good, even if they made a mistake.

Situation 3: School

A teacher may want all students to do well, but sometimes they cannot give everyone equal attention. Their intention is to help, but their competence is limited by time and resources.

In all these cases, looking at intention and competence separately helps you understand people better and keeps trust alive.

14.7 Activities to Practice Trust

Try these simple activities to understand and build trust in your relationships:

1. **Think of a recent mistake someone made.** Ask yourself: Was their intention good? Did they lack skill or knowledge?
2. **Talk to a friend or family member.** Share how you feel about trust. Listen to their thoughts and experiences.
3. **Write about a time you made a mistake.** Did others understand your intention? How did it make you feel?
4. **Help someone learn a new skill.** Notice how supporting each other builds trust.

14.8 Key Points to Remember

- Trust is believing that others want good for you.
- Intention is about what someone wants to do; competence is about what they can do.
- Most people have good intentions, even if they make mistakes.
- Do not judge others harshly for their lack of skill. Try to see their intention.
- Open communication, honesty, forgiveness, and support help build strong trust.
- Trust takes time to grow but can be lost quickly if we misunderstand each other.

14.9 Reflection Questions

1. Do I usually look at people's intentions or only their actions?
2. When someone makes a mistake, do I get angry or try to understand their intention?
3. How do I feel when someone trusts me, even if I make mistakes?
4. What can I do to build more trust in my relationships?
5. How can I help others improve their competence without hurting their feelings?

By understanding the difference between intention and competence, and by practicing trust, you can build stronger, happier, and more meaningful relationships with everyone around you.

Chapter 15: Understanding Respect and Differentiation

Recognizing the Inherent Value in Every Human Being

CHAPTER 15

UNDERSTANDING RESPECT AND DIFFERENTIATION

RECOGNIZING THE NEED FOR RESPECT

INTRODUCTION: THE NEED FOR RESPECT

- Recognition
- Acceptance
- Dignity
- Equal treatment

Respect acknowledges
the inherent worth of every individual

WHAT IS RESPECT?

- Honoring the innate value of every human being
- Universal and unconditional
- Basis for trust and cooperation

WHAT IS DIFFERENTIATION?

- Judging based on external factors like wealth or status
- Leads to hierarchy and division

Causes conflict and inequality

RESPECT vs.		DIFFERENTIATION
Basis	Honoring the innate value of every human	Extcach rese:talationship — Conflict, resentatn, jolation — Conflict, resemtance
Equality	Universal and uncoditional	Conflict, resentant and ulation Erosion vs resentijem

PRACTICING RESPECT IN DAILY LIFE

1. Recognize inherent equality
2. Listen without judgment
3. Speak mindfully
4. Acknowledge contributions

15.1 Introduction: The Need for Respect

Every human being has a natural desire for:

- Recognition
- Acceptance
- Dignity
- Equal treatment

This universal need is fulfilled through **respect** — an essential value that acknowledges the **inherent worth** of every individual, regardless of external markers like wealth, status, or background.

Yet, in today's world, respect is often misunderstood or replaced by **differentiation** — a mindset that ranks people based on superficial attributes. This chapter aims to:

- Clarify the **meaning of true respect**
- Contrast it with **differentiation**
- Offer strategies to **cultivate respectful behavior** in daily life

15.2 What is Respect?

Respect (Samman) means **recognizing and honoring the innate value of every human being** simply because they are human.

It is based on the understanding that:

- Every human being desires to live in harmony
- Each person has the capacity to understand and live in harmony
- No one is inherently inferior or superior

Respect is not something earned through achievement — it is something every person inherently deserves by virtue of being human.

15.2.1 Characteristics of Respect

Feature	Explanation
Universal	Applies to all humans, regardless of differences
Unconditional	Not based on performance, possessions, or prestige
Foundational	Basis for trust, affection, and cooperation

Internal	Arises from right understanding, not social pressure

15.2.2 Common Misconceptions about Respect

- "I only respect those who respect me first."
- "Respect must be earned."
- "You must prove yourself to deserve respect."

These ideas confuse **respect with admiration or reward.** While admiration is based on accomplishments, **respect is inherent and equal.**

15.3 What is Differentiation?

Differentiation is the **tendency to judge people as superior or inferior** based on external factors such as:

- Wealth
- Position or job title
- Education level
- Gender or race
- Religion or culture
- Physical appearance

Differentiation leads to comparison, inequality, and ultimately, social disharmony.

15.3.1 Examples of Differentiation in Everyday Life

- Giving more attention to a well-dressed guest than a modestly dressed one
- Valuing someone's opinion more because they are in a higher position
- Believing men are more capable in leadership roles
- Mocking someone's accent or physical appearance

These subtle behaviors damage relationships, breed resentment, and perpetuate inequality.

15.3.2 Effects of Differentiation

Effect on the Individual	**Effect on Society**

Loss of self-worth	Discrimination and exclusion
Feelings of inferiority/superiority	Conflict, misunderstanding
Dependence on approval	Hierarchical thinking
Constant competition	Erosion of mutual happiness and cooperation

15.4 Respect vs. Differentiation: A Clear Contrast

Aspect	Respect	Differentiation
Basis	Inherent human value	External attributes (status, wealth, etc.)
Equality	All humans are equally worthy	Creates hierarchy and division
Impact	Mutual happiness, cooperation	Conflict, resentment, and inequality
Expression	Acceptance, compassion, understanding	Prejudice, labeling, judgment

15.5 Practicing Respect in Daily Life

15.5.1 How to Cultivate Respect

1. **Recognize Inherent Equality**
    - Every person has potential and dignity
2. **Listen Without Judgment**
    - Accept people's perspectives, even if you disagree
3. **Speak Mindfully**
    - Avoid sarcasm, insults, or belittling tones
4. **Acknowledge Contributions**
    - Appreciate others' efforts, regardless of results
5. **Avoid Comparisons**
    - Each person's journey is unique and valuable

15.5.2 Respect in Different Relationships

Relationship	Respectful Behavior

Family	Valuing opinions of all members, including elders and children
Friends	Accepting differences without ridicule
Teachers/Students	Equal regard for learning and contribution
Workplace	Treating every role as vital, regardless of rank

15.6 Real-Life Scenarios: Respect vs. Differentiation

Scenario 1: Classroom Interaction

A student from a rural background speaks in broken English. Some classmates giggle, others avoid sitting with him.

- **Differentiation:** Judging based on language proficiency
- **Respect:** Valuing the student's willingness to learn and participate

Scenario 2: Family Decisions

The youngest sibling gives an idea at the dinner table, but it is ignored because they're "too young to understand."

- **Differentiation:** Dismissing based on age
- **Respect:** Listening to the idea without bias

Scenario 3: Workplace Inclusion

A junior staff member proposes a new system for efficiency. A senior dismisses it saying, "You don't have enough experience."

- **Differentiation:** Ranking based on position
- **Respect:** Evaluating the idea on its merit

15.7 Practice Session: Self-Awareness on Respect and Differentiation

Objective:

To help learners reflect on where they practice respect and where they might unconsciously differentiate.

Activity: Respect Reflection Log

Step 1: Think of 5 people you regularly interact with.

Step 2: Reflect and write:

- Do I value this person equally, regardless of their status or role?

- Have I ever dismissed or judged them based on external factors?
- What would respectful behavior look like in this relationship?

Respect Evaluation Table:

Person	My Behavior	Differentiation Indicators	Respectful Action I Can Take
Roommate	Often interrupt in conversations	Think their ideas are immature	Practice active listening
Classmate	Avoid asking for help	Assume they won't know the answer	Ask and appreciate input
Housekeeping staff	Barely acknowledge	Focus only on task, not the person	Greet by name and thank them

Group Sharing:

Encourage participants to share:

- A time they felt disrespected
- A time they unintentionally disrespected someone
- What they learned from this reflection

15.8 Respect as a Catalyst for Social Harmony

Respect is a powerful force for:

- Bridging gaps between people
- Fostering inclusion
- Enabling dialogue across differences
- Creating emotionally safe environments

When practiced collectively, respect forms the **foundation of an undivided and cooperative society**.

15.9 Summary of Key Learnings

- **Respect** is recognition of a person's innate value, independent of their external achievements.

- **Differentiation** is the source of most social conflict — based on judgment, comparison, and labeling.
- Respect can be **consciously cultivated** through listening, equality, and compassion.
- Real-life scenarios offer countless opportunities to **replace judgment with understanding**.
- Self-reflection helps us move from differentiation to true, universal respect.

15.10 Reflection Questions

1. What qualities do I currently base my respect for others on?
2. Have I ever felt disrespected because of how I look, speak, or where I come from?
3. Do I tend to value people more because of their role or title?
4. How do I behave differently with someone I consider "below" me?
5. What is one daily habit I can adopt to treat all people with equal respect?

Chapter 16: Harmony in Society – Resolution, Prosperity, Fearlessness, and Co-existence

The Comprehensive Goals of a Harmonious Social Order

Chapter 16: Harmony in Society – Resolution, Prosperity, Fearlessness, and Co-existence

The Comprehensive Goals of a Harmonious Social Order

16.1 Introduction: The Need for Social Harmony

Human beings are inherently social – we live in families, communities, institutions, and nations, indivɛdl-being is intértwined with the quality of relationghips and structures around us.

This chapter presents a framework to understand and realize four compeheni-sive human goals at the societal level:

A core prepechensíve thayğoaal to understand and

- Four comprehensive human gols
- Fearleśsness (itruśt) irésiv

16.2 Understanding the Four Goals of Social Harmony

16.2.1 Resolution in Individual

Resolution (Samodhan)

- Clarity in thought
- Inner harmony
- Stability in decɔision-making

16.2.3 Prosperity in the Family

Ibo individual with resolaten

- Basic in thafeiency
- No greed or insecurity
- Resources are shared, no hɐaɨoɐd
- Mutual care and gratilude

16.2.3 Fearlessness in Society

Fearlessness (Abhay) is a social ɐniol-onment free of threats, discrimination, and domination

Characteristics of a Fearless Society

- Everyone feels safe– physically
- People not judged based ason caste, gender, class, or religion
- Conflicts are resolved througlogue not Violence

16.2.4 Co-existence with Nature

The expending orels of Harmony

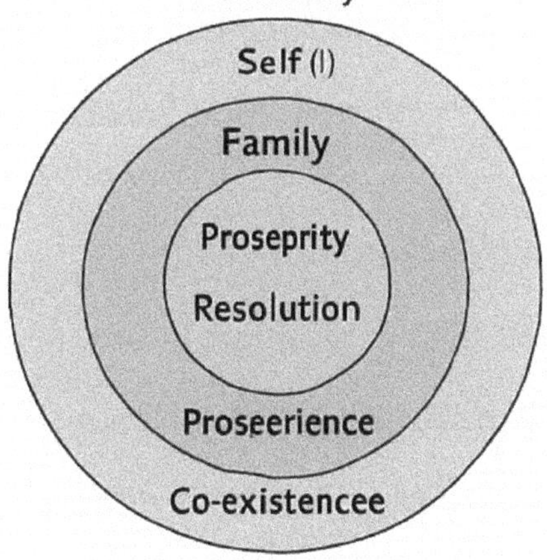

16.3 The Interconnectedness of the Four Goals

These goals are not isolated— they are interdependent:

1. Resolution in every y-individual leds to wise action

   Individuals are eroped a soonêtaaté

2. Become a pillar of trust and guiddance

   Uplnidds others through calm and clarity Sustainable co-existence

16.1 Introduction: The Need for Social Harmony

Human beings are inherently **social** — we live in families, communities, institutions, and nations. Our well-being is intertwined with the **quality of relationships and structures** around us. Individual happiness and societal health are deeply linked.

A harmonious society is **not just free of conflict**, but one in which individuals and systems actively support:

- Right understanding
- Mutual respect
- Shared prosperity
- Fearlessness
- Sustainable coexistence

This chapter presents a framework to understand and realize **four comprehensive human goals** at the societal level:

1. **Resolution in every individual**
2. **Prosperity in every family**
3. **Fearlessness (Trust) in society**
4. **Co-existence with nature**

16.2 Understanding the Four Goals of Social Harmony

16.2.1 Resolution in the Individual

Resolution (Samadhan) refers to:

- Clarity in thought
- Inner harmony
- Stability in decision-making

An individual with resolution is **self-aware**, **purpose-driven**, and contributes meaningfully to society.

Signs of a Resolved Individual:

- Free from confusion and contradiction
- Makes decisions based on holistic understanding
- Lives in alignment with values
- Maintains balanced emotions and relationships

Role in Society:

- Becomes a pillar of trust and guidance
- Uplifts others through calm and clarity

16.2.2 Prosperity in the Family

Prosperity (Samridhi) is not wealth alone — it is the **feeling of having enough** and the **capacity to share**.

Prosperity = **Physical sufficiency + Psychological contentment**

Indicators of a Prosperous Family:

- Basic needs are met with ease
- No greed or insecurity
- Resources are shared, not hoarded
- Mutual care and gratitude prevail

In contrast: Accumulation without contentment leads to tension and competition.

Societal Impact:

- Reduces inequality
- Promotes mutual support
- Discourages exploitation

16.2.3 Fearlessness in Society

Fearlessness (Abhay) is a **social environment free of threats**, discrimination, and domination.

It is the outcome of trust in human intention and respect for human dignity.

Characteristics of a Fearless Society:

- Everyone feels safe — physically, emotionally, and socially
- People are not judged based on caste, gender, class, or religion
- Conflicts are resolved through dialogue, not violence

Achieved through:

- Trust-based relationships
- Justice and fairness

- Participatory institutions
- Ethical leadership

16.2.4 Co-existence with Nature

Co-existence (Sah-Astitva) is a **state of mutual fulfillment** between humans and nature.

Nature provides all material needs; humans must engage **responsibly and reciprocally**.

Manifestations of Co-existence:

- Living with environmental sensitivity
- Using resources mindfully
- Conserving biodiversity
- Adopting eco-friendly technology

Without Co-existence:

- Pollution, climate change, and exploitation become inevitable

16.3 The Interconnectedness of the Four Goals

These four are not isolated — they are **interdependent**:

- **Resolution** in individuals → leads to wise action
- → **Prosperity** in families → removes fear-based behaviors
- → **Fearlessness** in society → nurtures collective well-being
- → **Co-existence** with nature → sustains life for all

Visual Model: The Expanding Circles of Harmony

1. **Self (I)** → Resolution
2. **Family** → Prosperity
3. **Society** → Fearlessness
4. **Nature** → Co-existence

Each layer builds upon the previous — starting from the **individual's inner clarity**.

16.4 Barriers to Social Harmony

1. Individual Conflicts

- Unresolved emotions, confusion, impulsiveness
- Leads to selfish or destructive behavior

2. Family Discontent

- Competition for wealth, lack of time or gratitude
- Leads to breakdown in relationships

3. Social Division

- Casteism, religious intolerance, gender bias
- Fear, insecurity, and injustice thrive

4. Environmental Abuse

- Overuse of resources, pollution, deforestation
- Future generations are put at risk

16.5 Real-Life Scenarios: Applying the Four Goals

Scenario 1: College Campus Conflict

- Clashes arise between student groups of different cultures
- Resolution: Facilitate dialogue and cultural exchange programs
- Outcome: Mutual understanding and fearlessness

Scenario 2: A Family in Debt

- Constant financial pressure leads to stress and blame
- Resolution: Assess needs vs. wants, live within means
- Outcome: Emotional balance and prosperity

Scenario 3: A Green Village Initiative

- Community adopts solar panels and bans plastic
- Result: Cleaner environment, reduced costs, inspired youth
- Co-existence becomes a collective value

16.6 Practice Session: Self and Society Reflection

Objective:

To reflect on one's role in contributing to social harmony.

Activity: Social Harmony Journal

Step 1: Self-Assessment Table

Area	My Current State	Desired State	Steps to Achieve
Personal Clarity	Often confused under stress	Make grounded decisions	Daily reflection, value education
Family Prosperity	Resources are sufficient	Feel less financial stress	Gratitude, needs assessment
Fearlessness	Avoid expressing views openly	Be able to share honestly	Build trust, non-judgmental spaces
Nature Connection	Overuse gadgets, waste water	Live more eco-responsibly	Conserve, recycle, educate peers

Step 2: Group Discussion Topics

- What's one thing I can do to reduce fear in my community?
- How can I help my family feel more prosperous?
- What would a university in co-existence with nature look like?

16.7 Roles of Institutions in Social Harmony

1. Educational Institutions

- Value-based curriculum
- Inclusive and democratic governance
- Encourage critical thinking and empathy

2. Workplaces

- Ethical leadership and fair practices
- Work-life balance and employee well-being
- Sustainability in business operations

3. Government and Law

- Policies based on equality and justice
- Transparent processes

- Access to basic needs for all

4. Media

- Promote respectful and constructive narratives
- Avoid fear-mongering and sensationalism

16.8 Vision of an Undivided Society and Universal Order

Undivided Society (Akhanda Samaj)

- Free of fragmentation by religion, caste, gender, class
- Built on understanding, not fear
- People live with mutual responsibility

Universal Human Order (SarvabhaumVyavastha)

- A world order where peace, prosperity, and sustainability are common goals
- Every individual and institution aligned with these values

16.9 Summary of Key Learnings

- Social harmony is a state where **individuals and institutions function in coherence**, driven by values.
- The **four universal goals** — resolution, prosperity, fearlessness, and co-existence — represent a holistic framework for a just society.
- Barriers like **mistrust, greed, fear, and exploitation** must be consciously addressed.
- Each person has a **role to play**, beginning with self-awareness and right understanding.
- Educational, political, and economic systems must support these values to build **a truly harmonious world**.
-

16.10 Reflection Questions

1. What does a harmonious society mean to me?
2. How do I contribute to fearlessness or fear in my environment?
3. Do I differentiate between prosperity and accumulation?
4. In what ways can I live in better co-existence with nature?
5. What small change can I make this week to promote resolution in myself or others?

Chapter 17: A Vision of Universal Human Order

Undivided Society and the Practice of Trust and Gratitude

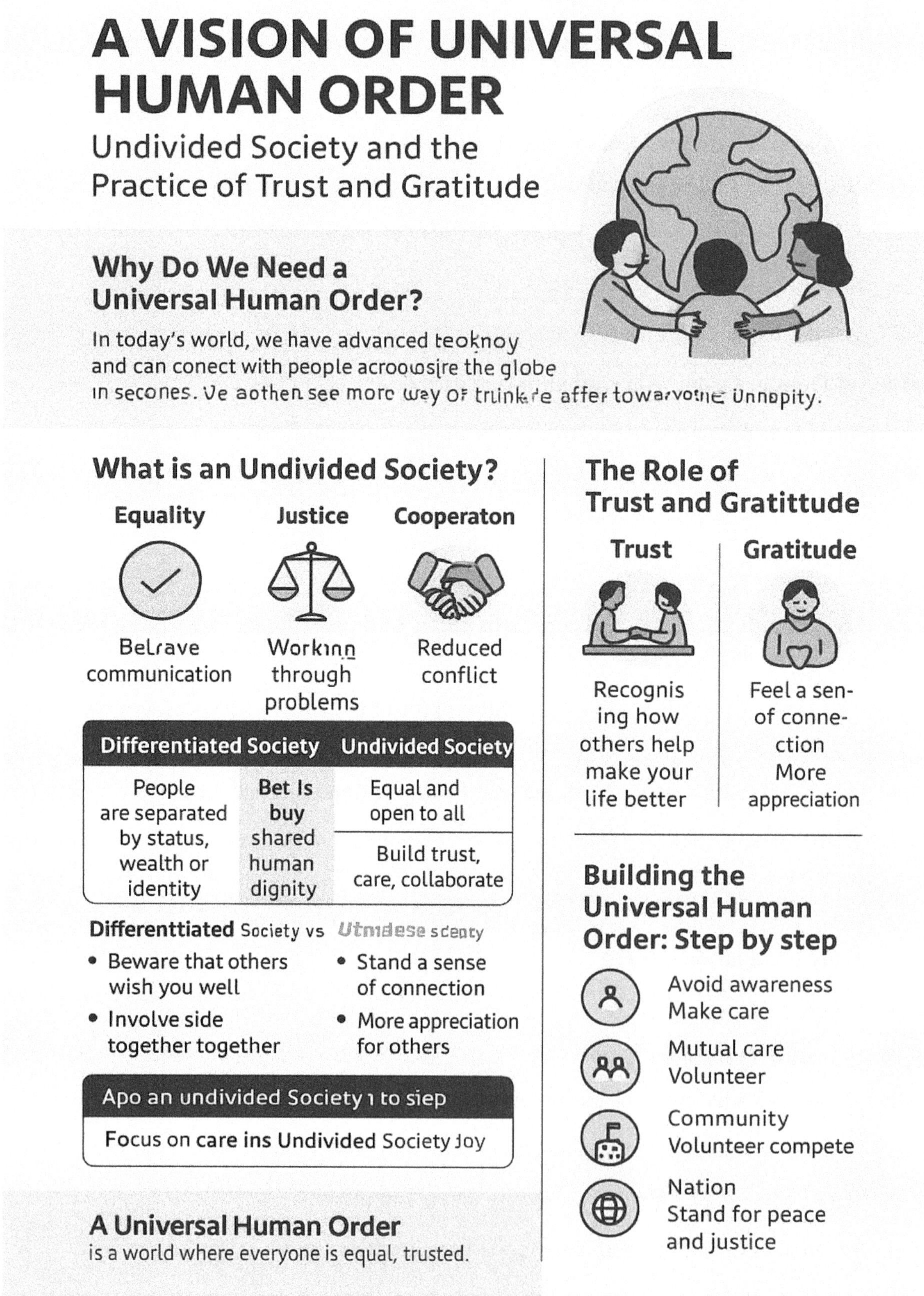

17.1 Introduction: Why Do We Need a Universal Human Order?

In today's world, we have advanced technology and can connect with people across the globe in seconds. Yet, we often see more fighting, unfairness, and separation. People are divided by money, religion, race, and nationality. Many feel left out, afraid, or unhappy. Even the environment is suffering because of how we live.

The answer is not just better rules or new leaders. We need a new way of thinking-a change in how we see ourselves and others. The idea of a **Universal Human Order** is about living together peacefully, with respect, fairness, and care for everyone. It starts with each person and family, then spreads to the whole world. In this vision, no one is left out or looked down upon. Trust and gratitude become part of daily life.

17.2 What is an Undivided Society?

17.2.1 Definition

An **Undivided Society** is a community where:

- Every person is seen as equal and valuable.
- There is no unfair treatment based on caste, religion, gender, wealth, or country.
- Systems and rules are fair and include everyone.
- People trust each other, not fear each other.

17.2.2 Features of an Undivided Society

Characteristic	Description
Equality	Everyone is treated with the same respect, no matter who they are.
Justice	Everyone gets fair treatment, without bias or prejudice.
Security	People feel safe and are free from fear or harm.
Cooperation	People help each other instead of competing.
Inclusiveness	Everyone has a place and a voice in society.

17.2.3 Differentiation vs. Unity

Differentiated Society	Undivided Society
People are separated by status, wealth, or identity	People are united by shared human dignity
Hierarchical and exclusive	Equal and open to all
Leads to mistrust and conflict	Builds trust, care, and teamwork
Focus on outside differences	Focus on inner values and abilities

17.3 The Role of Trust and Gratitude in the Universal Human Order

17.3.1 Trust

Trust means believing that others want good for you, just as you want good for them. It is about seeing that all people wish to live peacefully and happily. If someone behaves badly, it is usually because they do not understand, not because they want to harm you.

When trust is present:

- People talk openly.
- Problems are solved together.
- There is less fighting and more helping.

17.3.2 Gratitude

Gratitude means being thankful for what others do for you, and for how you are connected to the world. It is about noticing the small and big ways people and nature help you every day. Gratitude helps you feel humble and connected, instead of thinking you deserve everything by yourself.

When you practice gratitude:

- You appreciate others more.
- You feel happier and more connected.
- You want to give back and help others.

17.3.3 From Intention to Action

When you understand and practice trust and gratitude:

- You feel more peaceful inside.
- Relationships and communities become stronger.
- People act more responsibly and kindly.
- Schools, workplaces, and governments can improve.

17.4 Building the Universal Human Order: Step by Step

Level	What You Can Do
Individual	Become aware of your thoughts and feelings. Try to solve your own doubts and fears.
Family	Share tasks, listen to each other, and care for everyone.
Community	Volunteer, respect all types of work, and create spaces where everyone feels welcome.

Nation	Support fairness, respect diversity, and help make good laws.
World	Stand for peace, justice, and care for the environment everywhere.

17.5 Practice Session: Role-Playing Trust and Gratitude in Real Scenarios

Let's practice how to use trust and gratitude in real life. These activities help you move from just knowing about these values to actually living them.

Activity 1: Rebuilding Trust After Misunderstanding

Scenario:
Two friends had a fight because one felt ignored, while the other was just stressed.

Roles:

- Person A: Felt ignored
- Person B: Was overwhelmed
- Observer: Watches and gives feedback

Instructions:

- Each person thinks about what they really wanted.
- They talk using kind words, sharing their feelings honestly.
- The observer notices how the talk changes as they try to rebuild trust.

Debrief:

- How did trust break down?
- What helped fix it?
- What did you learn about misunderstanding and intention?

Activity 2: Expressing Gratitude to an Unnoticed Helper

Scenario:
Pick someone whose work you rarely thank (like a bus driver, cleaner, or cook).

Task:

- Write or say a thank-you message.
- Mention how their work helps your life.
- Notice how you feel before and after.

Sharing:

- How did the person react?

- How did you feel?
- What did you learn about the importance of saying thanks?

Activity 3: Group Circle – Web of Interdependence

Instructions:

- Sit in a circle.
- Each person names someone who helps them indirectly (like a farmer, electrician, or delivery person).
- Pass a ball of yarn or string to the next person as you name your helper.
- Soon, you'll see a web connecting everyone.

Reflection:

- How does this web show how we all depend on each other?
- How can you show more gratitude in daily life?
- What does it mean to live as part of a world family?

17.6 Reflection: What Would a Harmonious World Look Like?

Imagine a world where:

- People from different backgrounds live together without fear.
- Schools teach kindness before competition.
- Leaders are honest and serve everyone.
- Nature is cared for and shared fairly.

Now ask yourself:

- What can I do to help make this real?
- What small habit can I start today to live this vision?

17.7 Summary of Key Learnings

- A Universal Human Order is about a world where everyone is equal, trusted, and included.
- An Undivided Society means no one is left out or treated unfairly.
- Trust comes from understanding others' intentions, not just judging their actions.
- Gratitude helps us feel connected and humble.

- Practicing trust and gratitude in real life makes these values stronger.
- Change starts with you, but it can grow to your family, community, country, and the world.

17.8 Reflection Questions

- Do I usually trust that others mean well, or do I doubt them?
- Who in my life do I often forget to thank? Can I thank them today?
- What does "living in trust" look like for me?
- How can I help create an undivided society at my school or in my neighborhood?
- How would my day change if I acted with more gratitude?

By understanding and practicing these ideas, you can help create a world where everyone belongs, everyone is respected, and everyone is happy.

Chapter 18: Nature's Harmony and Interdependence

Nature's Harmony and Interdependence

Nature forms the foundation of our life, Understanding its harmony helps us to align our lives in sync with it.

The Four Orders in Nature

Material	Plant/Bio	Animal	Human

Soil, water. air, sunlight, rocks, etc.	Trees, plants, grasses, etc,	Birds, insects, mammals, etc.	All human beings

How the Four Orders Depend on Each Other

Nature's automatic balances:

- → Trees stop growing after a certain height
- → Animals hunt only as much as needed
- → Plants balance gases in the atmosphere

Humans have the ability and responsibility to care for all oher orders

Humans have the ability and responsibility to care for all other orders

Message from Nature: Enough for Need, Not for Greed

Nature provides enough to fulfill everyone's needs, not to satisfy endless demands.

Summary of Key Learnings

- → Nature is composed of four orders
- → All orders are interconnected
- → Nature maintains harmony by itself

18.1 Introduction: Why Harmony with Nature Matters

Nature is not just something outside our window-it is the base of our life. Everything we use, eat, drink, and breathe comes from nature. But today, many people forget how deeply we depend on nature. We often take more than we give back, and this causes problems like pollution, climate change, and loss of animals and plants.

To live well and happily, we must understand that nature is not just a collection of things. It is a system where everything is connected and balanced. When we understand this, we can learn to live in harmony with nature, not against it.

18.2 The Four Orders in Nature

Nature is organized into four main groups, called "orders." Each order has its own role and is important for the balance of the whole system.

1. Material Order

- **What it includes:** Soil, water, air, sunlight, rocks, metals, and other non-living things.
- **Role:** Provides the base for life. Supplies minerals, energy, and support for plants and animals.

2. Plant/Bio Order

- **What it includes:** Trees, plants, grasses, crops, algae.
- **Role:** Uses sunlight, water, and soil to grow. Produces food and oxygen. Helps keep the air and water clean.

3. Animal Order

- **What it includes:** All animals except humans-birds, insects, fish, mammals, reptiles.
- **Role:** Helps with pollination, spreads seeds, controls pests, and is part of the food chain. Animals react to nature but do not change it much.

4. Human Order

- **What it includes:** All human beings.
- **Role:** Can think, plan, and make choices. Can help maintain balance in nature or cause harm. Humans have the power and responsibility to protect and care for all orders.

18.3 How the Four Orders Depend on Each Other

None of these orders can exist alone. Each one gives and receives something from the others.

Order	Receives from	Gives to
Material	-	Minerals, energy, support
Plant	Material (soil, water)	Food, oxygen, shelter

Animal	Plants (food)	Pollination, soil health
Human	All three	Can protect or harm all orders

Nature is like a web, not a ladder. Humans are not "above" the others but are the most responsible because we can choose our actions.

18.4 Self-Regulation and Balance in Nature

Nature has its own ways to keep balance-this is called self-regulation. For example:

- Trees do not grow endlessly; they stop at a certain height.
- Animals hunt only as much as they need.
- Water cycles through rain, rivers, and clouds.
- Plants and animals keep the air clean by balancing oxygen and carbon dioxide.

These cycles keep nature healthy and balanced, without anyone controlling them.

What Happens When Humans Disturb This Balance?

When humans take too much or pollute, the balance is broken. This causes:

- Pollution of air, water, and soil
- Loss of plants and animals (extinction)
- Climate change
- Shortage of resources

18.5 Our Role: Living in Co-existence

Humans are different from other animals because we can think, reflect, and choose. We can either:

- Harm nature by being greedy and careless, or
- Live in harmony by understanding and respecting nature's balance

Co-existence means living in a way that supports all orders, not just ourselves. This includes:

- Using only what we need
- Giving back to nature (like planting trees)
- Reducing waste and pollution
- Supporting ways of living that are good for the environment

18.6 Nature's Message: Enough for Need, Not for Greed

Nature provides enough for everyone's basic needs. Problems start when we take more than we need or waste resources. If we use nature wisely and share, there is enough for all.

18.7 Practice Session: Observing and Understanding Nature's Harmony

Activity 1: Four Orders Walk

- Go for a walk in your area.
- Find and list:
    - 5 non-living things (rocks, water, air, metal, plastic)
    - 5 plants (trees, grass, flowers, crops, algae)
    - 5 animals (birds, insects, dogs, cows, fish)
    - 5 human-made things or actions (buildings, cars, people working)
- Observe how these things are connected. Are they in balance or not?

Activity 2: Nature Reflection Journal

Write about:

- One way you depend on each of the four orders every day.
- One habit you can change to help nature stay balanced.

Activity 3: Water Cycle Diagram

Draw a simple diagram showing:

- How water comes to your home
- How you use it
- Where it goes after use
- How you can save or reuse water

18.8 Summary of Key Learnings

- Nature is made up of four interconnected orders: Material, Plant, Animal, and Human.
- Each order depends on the others for balance and survival.
- Nature keeps itself balanced through cycles and self-regulation.
- Humans have the ability and responsibility to protect this balance.
- By making small, conscious choices, we can help restore and maintain harmony in nature.

18.9 Reflection Questions

1. What do I take from nature without giving back?
2. How does my lifestyle affect the other orders?
3. Can I think of one example of nature's self-regulation?

4. What is one habit I can change to support nature's harmony?
5. Do I see myself as part of nature or separate from it?

By understanding and respecting nature's harmony, we can live happier, healthier lives and help create a better world for everyone.

Chapter 19: Understanding Co-existence

Space as Universal Medium & Interaction of All Units

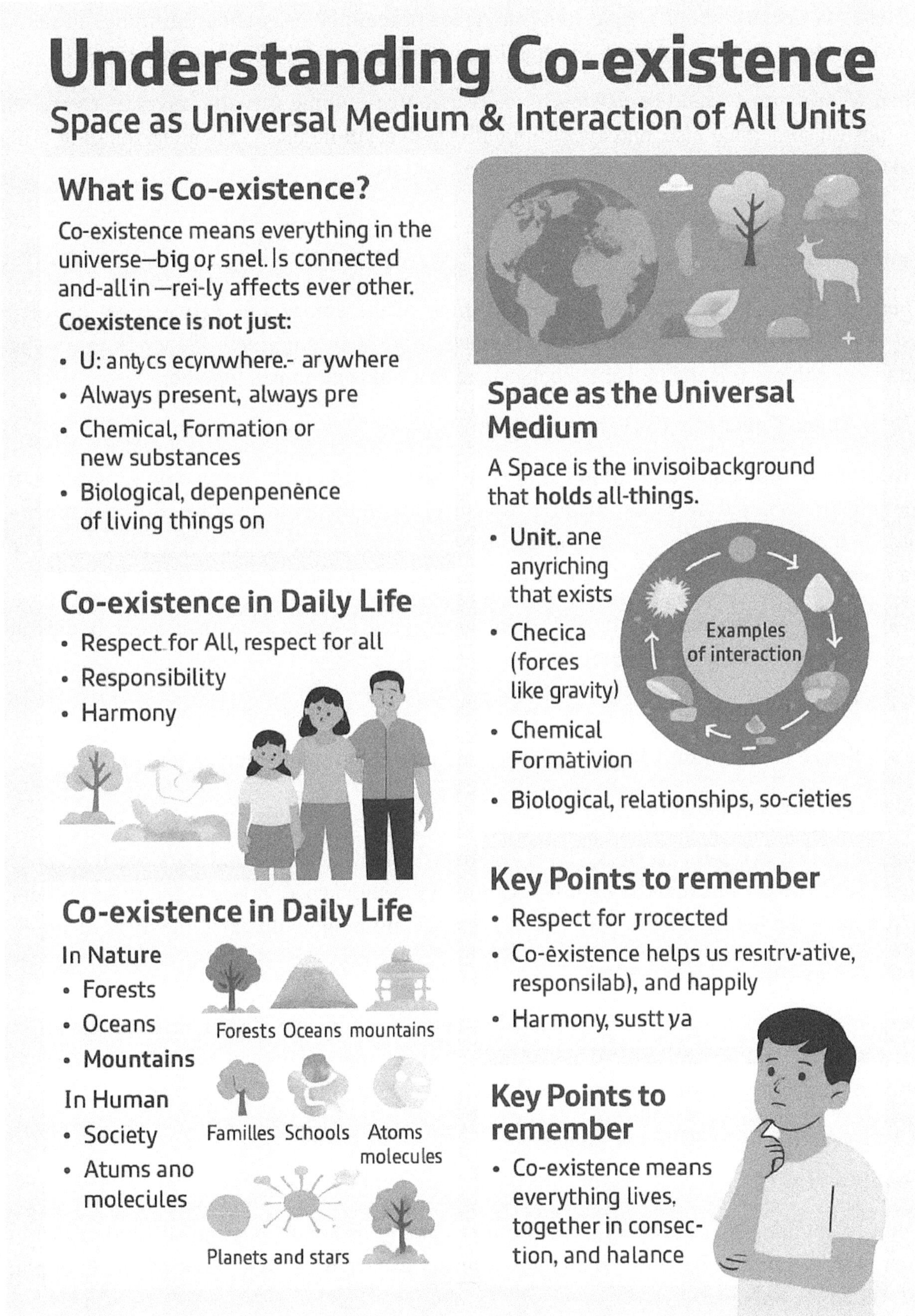

19.1 Introduction: What is Co-existence?

Co-existence means living together in harmony. It is the understanding that everything in the universe-big or small, living or non-living-exists together and is connected in some way. Co-existence is not just about people living together peacefully; it is about all things in nature, from tiny atoms to huge galaxies, sharing the same universe and affecting each other.

When we truly understand co-existence, we realize that nothing is really separate. Everything depends on something else, and everything affects everything else. This understanding brings respect, care, and responsibility for the world around us.

19.2 Space as the Universal Medium

What is Space?

When we hear the word "space," we might think of the empty area between objects or the vast sky above us. But in reality, space is much more than emptiness. Space is everywhere and in everything. It is the invisible background that holds all things together.

Why is Space Called the Universal Medium?

A medium is something that allows things to exist and interact. For example, water is the medium for fish, and air is the medium for birds and humans to breathe. In the same way, space is the medium for everything in the universe-stars, planets, air, water, plants, animals, and even humans.

- **Space is everywhere:** It fills every gap, every corner, even inside our bodies and between the tiniest particles.
- **Space is always present:** Even when there is nothing else, space remains.
- **Space is not empty:** It allows energy and matter to move, interact, and exist.

Space and Everything in It

Everything that exists-rocks, trees, rivers, animals, humans, planets, and stars-occupies space. Even the air we breathe and the light we see travel through space. Space is the stage on which the drama of the universe takes place. Without space, nothing could exist, move, or change.

Space is Not Just "Out There"

Sometimes, we think of space as only being "out there" in the sky or in outer space. But space is also here, around us and inside us. There is space between the cells in our body, between people in a room, and between objects on a table. Space is everywhere.

19.3 Interaction of All Units in Space

What is a "Unit"?

A unit is anything that exists-living or non-living, big or small. A grain of sand, a drop of water, a tree, a bird, a human, a mountain, a planet-all are units. Each unit has its own place and role in the universe.

How Do Units Interact?

All units exist in space, and they interact with each other in many ways. These interactions can be physical, chemical, biological, or even social.

1. Physical Interactions:

Objects affect each other through forces like gravity, magnetism, and electricity. For example, the Earth's gravity pulls us down, and the sun's gravity keeps the planets in orbit.

2. Chemical Interactions:

Atoms and molecules combine and react to form new substances. For example, plants take in carbon dioxide and water and, with sunlight, make food and oxygen.

3. Biological Interactions:

Living things depend on each other for food, shelter, and survival. For example, bees pollinate flowers, and animals eat plants.

4. Social Interactions:

Humans interact with each other through communication, sharing, and working together. Our relationships, societies, and cultures are all examples of interaction.

Examples of Interaction in Space

- **The Sun and Earth:** The sun's light and heat travel through space to reach the Earth, making life possible.
- **Plants and Animals:** Plants give out oxygen; animals breathe it in and give out carbon dioxide, which plants use.
- **Rain and Rivers:** Water evaporates into the air, forms clouds, falls as rain, and flows in rivers-connecting the sky, land, and sea.
- **Human Activities:** When we build houses, grow crops, or use machines, we are interacting with the land, air, water, and other living things.

Everything is Connected

No unit exists alone. Every unit is part of a bigger system. The food we eat comes from plants, which need soil, water, and sunlight. The air we breathe is cleaned by trees. Even our thoughts and actions affect others around us.

When we understand this, we start to see the world as a web of connections, not as separate pieces. This is the heart of co-existence.

19.4 Co-existence in Daily Life

In Nature

- **Forests:** Trees, animals, birds, insects, and soil all depend on each other.

- **Oceans:** Fish, seaweed, water, and sunlight create a balanced system.
- **Mountains:** Rocks, plants, snow, and rivers interact to support life.

In Human Society

- **Families:** Each person plays a role-parents, children, elders-all need each other.
- **Schools:** Teachers, students, staff, and parents work together for learning.
- **Communities:** People share resources, ideas, and responsibilities.

In the Universe

- **Planets and Stars:** The movement of planets and stars affects tides, seasons, and climate.
- **Atoms and Molecules:** The smallest particles combine to make everything we see and use.

19.5 Why is Understanding Co-existence Important?

- **Respect for All:** When we see that everything is connected, we respect all forms of life and nature.
- **Responsibility:** We realize our actions affect others and the environment.
- **Harmony:** Co-existence brings peace, balance, and happiness.
- **Sustainability:** Only by living in harmony can we protect nature for future generations.

19.6 Practice Session: Observing Co-existence

Activity 1: Web of Life

- Draw a picture showing how plants, animals, water, air, and humans are connected.
- Show arrows to indicate who gives and who receives.
- Discuss: What happens if one part of the web is removed?

Activity 2: Space Around Us

- Sit quietly and notice the space around you-in the room, between objects, between people.
- Think: How does space allow everything to exist together without bumping into each other?
- Share your thoughts with a friend or class.

Activity 3: Chain of Interactions

- Pick an object you use every day (like a pencil or a glass of water).

- List all the things and people involved in making it possible for you to use that object.
- Reflect on how many units are connected through space to bring you that one thing.

19.7 Key Points to Remember

- Co-existence means everything lives together in connection and balance.
- Space is not empty; it is the universal medium that holds and connects all things.
- All units-living and non-living-exist and interact within space.
- Nothing is truly separate; everything is part of a larger system.
- Understanding co-existence helps us live more respectfully, responsibly, and happily.

19.8 Reflection Questions

1. Can you see examples of co-existence in your home or school?
2. How does space help everything exist together without conflict?
3. What happens when one part of a system is disturbed or removed?
4. How can you show more respect for the connections in nature and society?
5. What is one thing you can do to support co-existence in your daily life?

When we see ourselves as part of the whole, connected to everything through space, we start to live with greater care, kindness, and understanding. This is the true meaning of co-existence.

Chapter 20: Harmony at Every Level

Personal, Familial, Societal, Universal

Harmony at Every Level

Introduction

What is Harmony?

Harmony mearis living in lance, peace, and cooperction It is the feeling that everything is working together, swirkhout conflict or confusion. Harmony.is not just about music or art it is also about eur thoughts, actions, and relationships.

When over is important winthin ourselves, in society, and in the universe.

Personal Harmony

What is Personal Harmony?

As balance within yourself.

How to Achieve Personal Harmony

- Self-awareness
- Clarify of values
- Healthy habits
- Positive thinking
- Self-acceptance

Signs of personalal harmony

- Feel peaceful and focused
- Make decisions easily.
- Handle stress calinly
- Feel good about yourself

Home feels good about yourself

Famillal Harmony

What is Achieve Harmony?

Different people in a commmunity or country live together peacefully.

Signs of Achieve Societal Harmony

- Respect diversity,
- Justice and fairness
- Helping others
- Community spirit
- Non-violence

Sories of woumd. wealthy.

Signs of societal Harmony

- People feel safe respected in public
- Crime, fear, fearr, at and discrimination
- Communities being lean Joryful
- Asense of connection with the whole

Societal Harmony

As balance and connection between all living and non-living things in an

Steps to Achieve Societal Harmony

- Respect diversity
- Justice and fairness
- Helping others
- Community spirit
- Non-violence

Universal Harmony

As balance and connection between all living and non-living things in the em.

Signs of Universal Harmony

- Clean and healthy ı hetalthy
- Animals and plants thrive alongside humans
- Natural digasters are less conmen duro balanced living
- There is a connenction with the whole world

20.1 Introduction: What is Harmony?

Harmony means living in balance, peace, and cooperation. It is the feeling that everything is working together smoothly, without conflict or confusion. Harmony is not just about music or art-it is also about our thoughts, actions, and relationships. When there is harmony, life feels joyful, meaningful, and secure.

Harmony is important at every level of our lives: within ourselves, in our families, in society, and in the whole universe. Let's explore what harmony looks like at each level and how we can achieve it.

20.2 Personal Harmony

What is Personal Harmony?

Personal harmony is the balance within yourself. It means your thoughts, feelings, and actions are in agreement. You feel calm, clear, and confident. You know what you want and why you want it. You are not always fighting with yourself or feeling pulled in different directions.

How to Achieve Personal Harmony

- **Self-awareness:** Understand your thoughts, feelings, and needs.
- **Clarity of values:** Know what is important to you.
- **Healthy habits:** Take care of your body and mind.
- **Positive thinking:** Focus on solutions, not just problems.
- **Self-acceptance:** Be kind to yourself and learn from mistakes.

Signs of Personal Harmony

- You feel peaceful and focused.
- You make decisions easily.
- You handle stress calmly.
- You feel good about yourself.

20.3 Familial Harmony

What is Familial Harmony?

Familial harmony is peace and understanding in your family. It means family members care for each other, share responsibilities, and solve problems together. There is love, trust, and respect among all.

How to Achieve Familial Harmony

- **Open communication:** Talk honestly and listen carefully.
- **Sharing and caring:** Help each other with daily tasks and feelings.

- **Respect for all:** Value every member, young or old.
- **Support:** Stand by each other in good and bad times.
- **Quality time:** Spend time together, celebrate, and create happy memories.

Signs of Familial Harmony

- Family members feel safe and loved.
- Arguments are solved peacefully.
- Everyone feels included and important.
- The home feels warm and welcoming.

20.4 Societal Harmony

What is Societal Harmony?

Societal harmony means different people in a community or country live together peacefully. There is cooperation, fairness, and respect, no matter what someone's background or beliefs are. People work together for the common good.

How to Achieve Societal Harmony

- **Respect diversity:** Accept differences in culture, religion, language, and ideas.
- **Justice and fairness:** Treat everyone equally and stand against injustice.
- **Helping others:** Support those in need and share resources.
- **Community spirit:** Take part in local events, volunteer, and build friendships.
- **Non-violence:** Solve conflicts with words, not fists.

Signs of Societal Harmony

- People feel safe and respected in public.
- There is less crime, fear, and discrimination.
- Communities are clean, healthy, and joyful.
- People trust and help each other.

20.5 Universal Harmony

What is Universal Harmony?

Universal harmony is the balance and connection between all living and non-living things in the universe. It means humans, animals, plants, earth, water, air, and even stars and planets exist together peacefully, each playing their part.

How to Achieve Universal Harmony

- **Care for nature:** Protect plants, animals, water, and air.

- **Use resources wisely:** Take only what you need and avoid waste.
- **See the big picture:** Understand that your actions affect the whole world.
- **Promote peace:** Wish for the well-being of all, not just yourself.
- **Learn from nature:** Notice how everything in nature works together and try to follow that example.

Signs of Universal Harmony

- The environment is clean and healthy.
- Animals and plants thrive alongside humans.
- Natural disasters are less common due to balanced living.
- There is a sense of connection with the whole world.

20.6 Practice Session: Bringing Harmony into Your Life

Activity 1: Personal Reflection

- Sit quietly and think: Are my thoughts, feelings, and actions in harmony? If not, what can I change?

Activity 2: Family Circle

- Gather your family. Each person shares one thing they appreciate about another member and one way the family can be more harmonious.

Activity 3: Community Action

- With friends or classmates, plan a small project to help your community (like cleaning a park, planting trees, or helping someone in need).

Activity 4: Nature Walk

- Go outside and observe how plants, animals, water, and air work together. Discuss how you can help keep this harmony.

20.7 Key Points to Remember

- Harmony is needed at every level: personal, familial, societal, and universal.
- It starts with self-awareness and grows outwards to include everyone and everything.
- Small actions, like kindness and respect, help build harmony everywhere.
- When there is harmony, life is happier, healthier, and more meaningful.

20.8 Reflection Questions

1. What does harmony mean to me?
2. Where do I see harmony in my life? Where is it missing?

3. What can I do today to create more harmony at home, in my school, and in nature?
4. How does harmony in one area (like family) affect other areas (like society)?
5. Why is universal harmony important for the future?

By understanding and practicing harmony at every level, we can create a better life for ourselves, our families, our communities, and the entire world. Harmony is the key to lasting happiness and peace.

Chapter 21: Environmental Imbalance: Human Responsibility

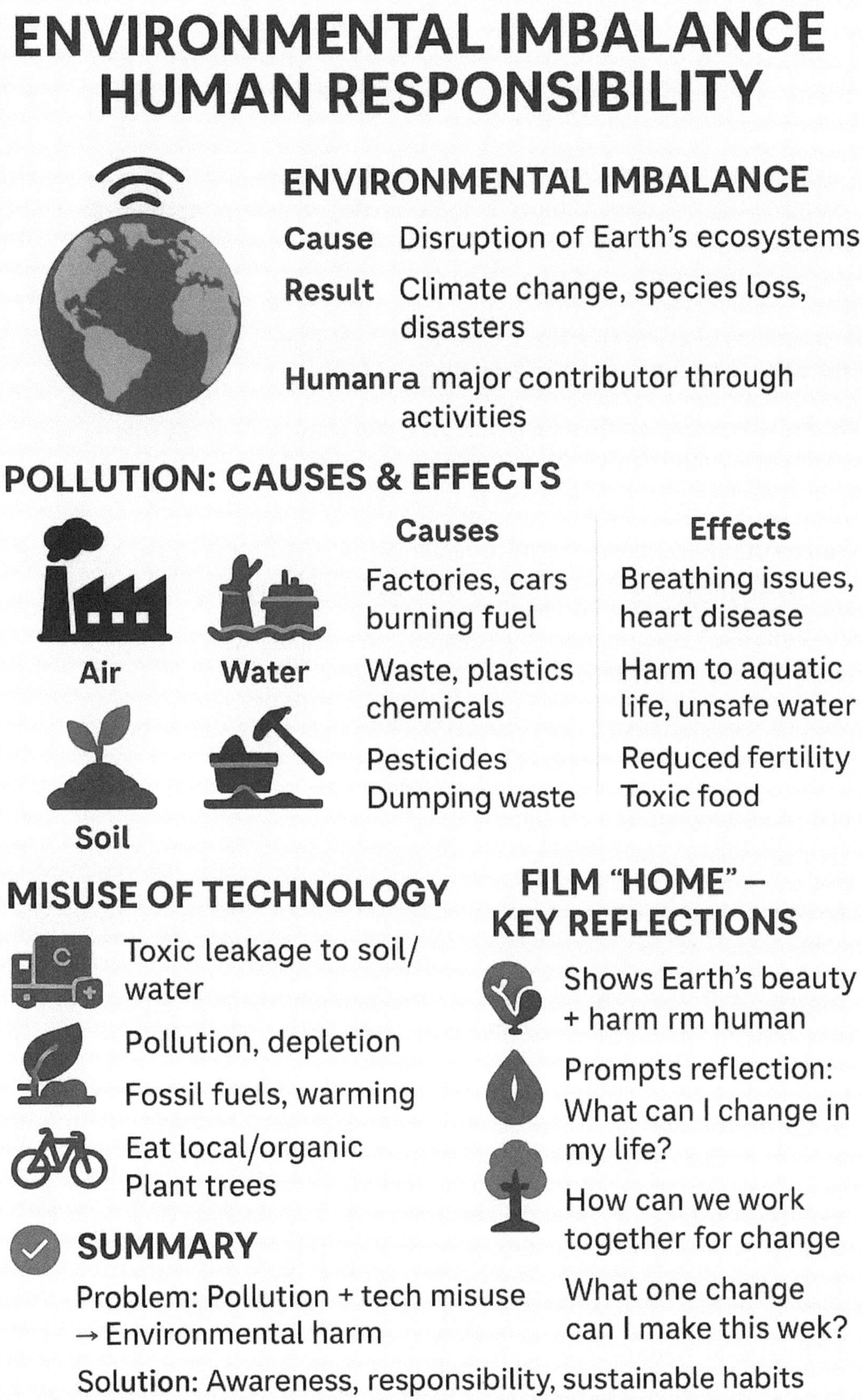

21.1 Understanding Environmental Imbalance

Environmental imbalance happens when the natural balance of the Earth's ecosystems is disturbed. This disturbance is often caused by human activities like pollution and the misuse of technology. When this balance is upset, it harms plants, animals, water, air, and even human health. It can lead to problems like climate change, loss of species, and natural disasters.

Humans have a special responsibility because many of these problems are caused by our actions. Recognizing this responsibility is the first step toward protecting the environment and restoring balance.

21.2 Pollution: Its Causes and Effects

Pollution means adding harmful substances to the environment. It can affect the air we breathe, the water we drink, and the soil that grows our food.

- **Air Pollution:** Smoke from factories, cars, and burning fuels fills the air with harmful gases and particles. This causes breathing problems, heart diseases, and can even lead to climate change by trapping heat in the atmosphere.
- **Water Pollution:** Chemicals, waste, and plastics thrown into rivers, lakes, and oceans poison aquatic life and make water unsafe for humans and animals.
- **Soil Pollution:** Using too many pesticides and dumping waste harms the soil, making it less fertile and contaminating food grown in it.

Pollution not only damages nature but also affects human health and livelihoods. It can cause diseases, reduce crop yields, and make living conditions difficult.

21.3 Misuse of Technology and Its Impact

Technology has brought many benefits, but when misused, it can harm the environment:

- **Electronic Waste:** Old phones, computers, and gadgets contain toxic materials. When thrown away carelessly, these poisons leak into soil and water.
- **Overuse of Resources:** Manufacturing technology requires mining minerals and using energy, often from fossil fuels, which increases pollution and resource depletion.
- **Energy Consumption:** Many technologies consume large amounts of electricity, much of which comes from polluting sources, adding to global warming.
- **Uncontrolled Growth:** Rapid urbanization and industrialization without proper planning lead to deforestation, loss of green spaces, and increased waste.

Using technology wisely means balancing progress with care for the environment.

21.4 Film Discussion: "Home"

The film "Home" shows beautiful images of Earth's natural wonders and the damage caused by human activities. It highlights how forests are cut down, rivers polluted, and animals losing their homes. The film urges us to think about how we live and what we can do to protect the planet.

Discussion Ideas:

- What parts of the film made you feel hopeful or worried?
- How does human activity affect nature in the film?
- What changes can we make in our lives to help the Earth?
- How can communities and governments work together for a healthier planet?

21.5 Practice Session: Reflecting on Sustainable Living

Sustainable living means making choices that protect the environment and use resources wisely so future generations can also enjoy a healthy planet.

Simple Ways to Live Sustainably:

- **Reduce waste:** Use less plastic, recycle, and avoid throwing things away unnecessarily.
- **Save energy:** Turn off lights and devices when not in use, use energy-efficient products.
- **Conserve water:** Fix leaks, take shorter showers, and use water carefully.
- **Choose eco-friendly transport:** Walk, cycle, or use public transport instead of private vehicles.
- **Support local and organic food:** It reduces pollution and supports healthy farming.
- **Plant trees and protect green spaces:** Trees clean the air and provide homes for animals.

Reflection Questions:

- What habits in my daily life help or harm the environment?
- What is one change I can make this week to live more sustainably?
- How does my family or community impact the environment?
- What can I do to encourage others to care for the planet?

21.6 Summary

Environmental imbalance is caused mainly by pollution and misuse of technology, both linked to human actions. These problems threaten the health of the planet and all living beings. Understanding our responsibility and making small, positive changes in how we live can help restore balance. Films like "Home" inspire us to appreciate the Earth's beauty and motivate us to protect it. Sustainable living is a practical way each of us can contribute to a healthier, happier planet.

By taking responsibility and acting with care, we can reduce environmental harm and create a better future for ourselves and all life on Earth.

Chapter 22: Natural Acceptance and Professional Ethics

22.1 Introduction: Why Values and Ethics Matter in Technical Education

In today's world, technology shapes every aspect of our lives. Engineers and professionals have the power to create, innovate, and solve problems-but their choices also affect society, the environment, and future generations. That's why it is essential for technical education to include not only technical knowledge but also strong human values and professional ethics. Natural acceptance means making choices that feel right deep within us, guided by our inner understanding of what is good for ourselves and others.

22.2 Values in Technical Education

Values are the guiding principles that help us distinguish right from wrong and make responsible decisions. In technical education, values are as important as technical skills. They ensure that engineers and professionals:

- Respect the rights and dignity of others
- Show honesty, integrity, and responsibility in their work
- Care for the well-being of society and the environment
- Are loyal to their profession and committed to continuous learning
- Tolerate diversity and accept different perspectives
- Use their knowledge for the common good, not just personal gain

By developing these values, students learn to deal with moral complexities, resolve ethical dilemmas, and justify their decisions with sound reasoning. This makes them not only skilled professionals but also responsible citizens.

22.3 Professional Ethics: What Does It Mean?

Professional ethics refers to the set of moral principles and standards that guide the behavior of professionals. For engineers, this includes:

- Recognizing and solving moral problems in their work
- Acting with fairness, honesty, and transparency
- Respecting safety, health, and welfare of the public
- Avoiding conflicts of interest and misuse of power
- Protecting confidential information
- Being open to feedback and continuous improvement

Professional ethics also means being willing to take responsibility for one's actions and decisions, even when it is difficult. It involves a commitment to act in ways that are morally right, reasonable, and in line with both personal and professional values.

22.4 Practice Session: Conduct of an Ethical Engineer

Scenario 1: Safety vs. Cost

An engineer discovers that a cheaper material could save money on a project, but it may not be as safe for users.

Ethical conduct: The engineer chooses safety over cost, informs the team of the risks, and recommends the safer material, even if it costs more.

Scenario 2: Honesty in Reporting

A team member makes a mistake in calculations, but no one else notices.
Ethical conduct: The engineer points out the error, corrects it, and makes sure the report is accurate, even if it means extra work or admitting a mistake.

Scenario 3: Respecting Diversity

A new colleague comes from a different background and has a different approach to problem-solving.
Ethical conduct: The engineer listens with respect, values the new perspective, and encourages teamwork, helping everyone learn from each other.

Scenario 4: Environmental Responsibility

A project could harm the environment if not managed carefully.
Ethical conduct: The engineer suggests eco-friendly solutions, follows environmental laws, and educates others about sustainable practices.

22.5 Reflection and Discussion

- Why is it important for engineers to act ethically, even when no one is watching?
- How do personal values influence professional decisions?
- Can you think of a real-life example where ethical conduct made a difference in a project or workplace?
- What challenges might arise in following professional ethics, and how can they be overcome?

22.6 Summary

Natural acceptance and professional ethics are at the heart of responsible technical education. By developing strong values and ethical habits, engineers and professionals can make decisions that benefit themselves, their organizations, society, and the world. Ethical conduct ensures trust, safety, and progress for all, making technology a force for good.

Eco-Friendly Technologies and Models

Introduction: Production Systems in Harmony

Eco-friendly technologies and production models are designed to meet human needs while protecting the environment and supporting social well-being.

These systems aim to reduce wàste, conserve resources, use renewable energy, and minimize pollution.

Production Systems in Harmony

1 Reducing Waste
Using recycling, cônnicLiein·processes and designng naste.

2 Energy Efficiency
Using reduction, and saving energy.

3 Renewable Energy
Water efficiency

4 Lean and Green Manufacturing
in reduce fewer (sarch

Practice Session: Design a People- and Eco-Friendly Product/Service

1. Form Smail Groups
2. Choose a Need
3. Brainstrom Solutions
   - Form small gróups: if imake ghr-o common probiem or need in your community (e g.
   - Cleán water, healthhy food, waste reduction, energy saving)
   - Brainstorm solutions; produce a product or service that solves eó?
   - How is it sâfe and accessible for everyone?

Real-World Case Studies

1 Additive Manufacturing (3D Printing)

Many manufacturets powering their plants with solat-wind, or hydro energy, reducing earyon emissions and saving money.

3 Circular Economy and COs Reuse

Capturing (arban diexide from industrial processes to máke new materialsr such as foams and plastics.

5 Algáe Biorefineries

integrating algáe production intò wastewater treatment plants to grow food.

5 Algae Biorefineries

Exàmples include.

- a rnusable water bytt k: made from recycled plastic, with a filter for ctean drinking water
- A solar-powered phone charger ding blodegradable

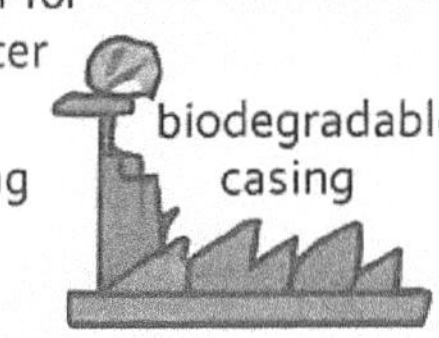

  A com muniry composting service
- A bike-sharing program to reduce car use and air pollution.

Summary

Eco-friendly technotogies and harmonious production

23.1 Introduction: Production Systems in Harmony

Eco-friendly technologies and production models are designed to meet human needs while protecting the environment and supporting social well-being. These systems aim to reduce waste, conserve resources, use renewable energy, and minimize pollution. The goal is to create products and services that are both people-friendly and planet-friendly, ensuring a better future for all.

23.2 Production Systems in Harmony

Modern sustainable production systems focus on:

- **Reducing Waste:** Using recycling, closed-loop processes, and designing products for reuse or composting to keep materials out of landfills.
- **Energy Efficiency:** Using equipment and machinery that require less energy, such as high-efficiency motors, LED lighting, and smart systems that optimize energy use.
- **Renewable Energy:** Powering factories and operations with solar, wind, or hydro energy to cut carbon emissions.
- **Sustainable Materials:** Choosing renewable, recycled, or biodegradable materials, such as bioplastics, PET, HDPE, or plant-based resources.
- **Water Conservation:** Treating and reusing water, and implementing water-efficient practices in manufacturing.
- **Lean and Green Manufacturing:** Streamlining processes to use fewer resources and produce less waste, often supported by digital monitoring and smart analytics.
- **Circular Economy Models:** Designing products and systems so that materials are reused, recycled, or returned safely to nature, closing the loop on resource use.

23.3 Real-World Case Studies

1. Additive Manufacturing (3D Printing)

3D printing is revolutionizing manufacturing by producing parts on-demand, reducing waste, and saving energy. Companies like Vestas (wind turbines) and Transaera (air conditioning) use 3D printing to make components closer to where they are needed, cutting down on shipping and material waste. For example, producing a scale model of an aircraft with 3D printing used much less energy and material compared to traditional methods.

2. Renewable Energy in Production

Many manufacturers now power their plants with solar, wind, or hydro energy. This shift not only reduces carbon emissions but also saves money and makes companies less dependent on fossil fuels. For example, some beverage companies have switched to renewable energy and improved machinery to cut electricity and gas use by 15%.

3. Circular Economy and CO_2 Reuse

In Europe, projects like EnCO2re are capturing carbon dioxide from industrial processes and using it to make new materials, such as foams and plastics. This approach reduces greenhouse gas emissions and creates valuable products from what was once waste.

4. Sustainable Agriculture and Food Production

Urban farms like Bowery Farming and Plenty use vertical farming and smart technology to grow food with less land, water, and chemicals. Techniques such as drip irrigation, biological pest control, and no-till farming help conserve resources and protect the environment in agriculture.

5. Algae Biorefineries

Innovative systems are integrating algae production into wastewater treatment plants. Algae capture CO_2 and clean water, and the resulting biomass can be used for animal feed, bioplastics, or biofuels, creating a closed-loop system that benefits both industry and nature.

23.4 Practice Session: Design a People- and Eco-Friendly Product/Service

Activity Steps

1. **Form Small Groups:** Work in teams of 3-5.
2. **Choose a Need:** Identify a common problem or need in your community (e.g., clean water, healthy food, waste reduction, energy saving).
3. **Brainstorm Solutions:** Think of a product or service that solves this problem while being kind to people and the environment.
4. **Design Features:** Consider:
    - What materials will you use? Are they renewable or recycled?
    - How will the product be made? Can you use local resources or renewable energy?
    - How will it reduce waste, pollution, or energy use?
    - How is it safe and accessible for everyone?
5. **Present Your Idea:** Share your design with the class, explaining how it benefits both people and the planet.

Example Ideas

- A reusable water bottle made from recycled plastic, with a filter for clean drinking water.
- A solar-powered phone charger using biodegradable casing.
- A community composting service that turns food waste into fertilizer for local gardens.
- A bike-sharing program to reduce car use and air pollution.

23.5 Reflection Questions

- How does your design help both people and the environment?
- What challenges did you face in making your product/service eco-friendly?
- How can these ideas be improved or scaled up in real life?
- Why is it important to consider both human and ecological needs in design?

23.6 Summary

Eco-friendly technologies and harmonious production systems are essential for a sustainable future. By learning from real-world examples and practicing creative design, we can develop solutions that protect the planet while meeting human needs. Everyone has a role to play in building a greener, more just world.

www.ingramcontent.com/pod-product-compliance
Ingram Content Group UK Ltd.
Pitfield, Milton Keynes, MK11 3LW, UK
UKHW061541190726
13845UKWH00031B/1152

9 789334 300635